MIGUEL'S TAPAS
a la Maestre

MIGUEL'S TAPAS
a la Maestre

Miguel Maestre

NEW HOLLAND

ACKNOWLEDGEMENTS

Thank you so much to my beautiful wife Sascha for all her love and support in everything I do in life. You have been instrumental in helping me write this book. For all the hours and hours of typing and fixing my grammar, I will never forget. You are the reason why I wake up every morning—you are my inspiration, my fuel and my energy. *Te quiero mucho.*

To my beautiful *hija* Claudia, the girl of my dreams. I dedicate this book to you as you are the most delicious dish I have ever cooked. *Te quiero mucho.*

To my Mama y Papa, Flora and Antonio, and brothers Antonio and Carlos, thank you for everything you have done for me. You are the best family in the world. *Os dedico este libro con todo mi amor de hijo, y el respeto y admiracion que tuve, tengo y tendre por vosotros los mejores padres del mundo.*

I would also like to say a big thank you to Sascha's family, Maggie, Hayley, Gary and Irene, for welcoming me with open arms when I arrived on the Australian shores, and for their continued love and support.

Also a huge *gracias* to my amazing TV family from our show 'The Living Room', Amanda, Chris and Barry. Working with you is a dream come true.

To the amazing team at New Holland, for your outstanding professionalism in every aspect of my book.

A huge thank you to Kellie-Marie Thomas for testing all the recipes and fixing all my grammatical errors, Trish Hegearty for her fabulous food styling and Karen Watson for all the beautiful photography.

And last but not least, a huge thank you to the best agents in the world Justine May and Tracy Gualano, for always being there for me. Since we first met until now we have achieved so much together and I am looking forward to many more years of success.

Miguel

CONTENTS

INTRODUCTION 12

BREAKFAST

Desayuno

6.30AM

Churros with Chocolate 28

Gypsy Arms with White Chocolate
Cream 30

7.00AM

Crispy Potato and Chorizo Egg 34

Flamenca Eggs 37

9.00AM

Caramelised Melon and Crispy Jamon
Iberico 40

10.00AM

Spanish Potato Omelette 45

5-Minute Spanish Potato Omelette 46

Rustic Zucchini Roast 51

Manchego Bread Rolls 54

MORNING TEA

Almuerzo

11.00AM

Calasparra Rice-Crusted Sardines 58

Kingfish Ceviche 62

Soft Shell Crab and Sauté of Edamame 67

Tuna Carpaccio with Tomato Sauce 70

12.00PM

Bechamel and Prawn Stuffed Mussels 73

Chorizo Cider Style 78

Garlic Prawns 83

Gazpacho from Andalucia 86

Spanish Ratatouille 89

Spanish Baked Beans 92

Bacalao Salted Cod Croquettes 95

White and Black Anchovy Skewers 100

LUNCH

Comida

1.00PM

Marinara-Style Rice 106

Creamed Aubergine 110

Vanilla Infused Wild Boar Cheeks 115

Pork Salad 116

2.00PM

Murcian Tuna Salad 121

Paella a la Maestre 124

Rabbit and Garlic Rice 128

Black Rice with Cuttlefish and Giant
Prawns 'Maestre Style' 134

Gypsy Vegetable Stew with Pears 139

Traditional Spanish Fish Broth 140

Roasted Potato Halves 144

Potato Fries 149

DESSERT

Postre

3.00PM

Heaven's Little Pig Caramel Delight	152
Lightly Fried Milk Pâttissier	155
Fresh Orange Set Custard	158
Bread and Butter Pudding	163
Creamy Cinnamon and Citrus Rice Pudding	166
Santiago's Tart	168

AFTERNOON TEA

Merienda

6.00PM

Duck Liver Pate	174
Galician-Style Octopus	179
Empanadillas	182
Wagyu and Chorizo Meat Pie	185
Sweet and Savoury Chicken Pie	188

DINNER

Cena

9.00 PM

Homemade Chorizo	194
Seafood Fideua	199
Chicken Cabbage Parcels	202
Veal Sweetbreads	206
Prawn Gow-Gee Spanish Style	210
Chickpea and Pork Hotpot	215
Lamb Shanks a la Española	218
Lamb Chops with Garlic	223
Marc Singla's Deconstructed Spanish Omelette	226

EVENING SNACKS

Picoteo Nocturno

3.00AM

Sweet Battered Lemon Leaves	232
Wild Rice Popcorn	237
Bombe Alaska Fruit Skewers	240
Chocolate Fondue with Strawberries Flambé	245
Fig Sorbet and Crispy Serrano	248
Manchego Cheese Sticks and Tomato Jam	253

BASICS & SAUCES

Basicos y Salsas

Grilled Sardines	258
Dry Tuna Fillet with Almonds	261
Chicken Stock	262
Brown Chicken Stock	263
Veal Stock	264
Lobster Stock	265
Parsley Oil	268
Basil Oil	269
Roast Garlic	270
Aioli	272
Lemon Vinaigrette	275
Black Olive Vinaigrette	276
Cava Vinaigrette	279
White Sauce with Giant Caperberries	280
Romesco Marinade	281
Sugar Syrup	282
Vanilla Custard	283
Crème Anglaise	285

GLOSSARY

GLOSSARY	286

Hola Amigos! We invite you to enjoy tapas [...] [...]ro Loco. We invite you to enjoy tapas [...] is fast, impulsive, fun just like our chef Miguel. [...] [...]etween three people and comes out of the kitchen as soon as [...] we suggest you order a few dishes, enjoy, then, order a few m[...] in Spain, if you don't like the food, drink more wine!

Tapas

de carrasca con aceite de oliva virgen organico
ead roll, organic extra virgin olive oil 'La Amarilla de R[...]

Olivas, manzanillas marinadas ala Murciana
selection of marinated manzanilla olives Murcian style

Patatas fritas con mayonesa
[...] chunky chips, mayonnaise

INTRODUCTION

I thank my lucky stars every day that I grew up in an area so rich in culinary tradition and plentiful produce—it most certainly planted the roots for the path I have followed today. Murcia is a beautiful coastal city in the south-east of Spain, resplendent with grand mountain ranges and numerous rivers running down to its sandy beaches.

It sits near the middle of a flat, fertile plain, with the Segura River running through the city from west to east. An ingenious irrigation system (for which the city is famous), started by the Romans and finished by the Moors, drip-feeds the land. This, combined with a climate of hot summers and mild winters, has given it a long history as an agricultural producer. Growing this abundant array of fruit, vegetables and flowers has generated its bountiful nickname of 'Europe's orchard'.

The agricultural countryside of Murcia is called *La Huerta* and yields, in my eyes, some of the most excellent produce in Spain. The Murcian people appreciate the wealth of fare available to them and over time have created dishes full of imagination and creativity, steeped in the flavours of the land.

As clichéd as it sounds, the motivation to explore and achieve, came directly from having grown up in a happy, loving environment. Flora and Antonio Luis, Mama y Papa, are as in love as the day they first met—a rare thing these days and something my brothers and I don't take for granted. This, and my mother's belief that family is the engine that keeps the wheels of life moving forward, certainly fostered an environment for all of us boys to believe in ourselves and follow our dreams.

My youngest brother, Carlos, followed me into the culinary world to study oenology (the science and study of winemaking) at university and became a sommelier. He is also a 'master of jamon'—the very serious business of producing, curing and carving Spain's famed answer to caviar.

My real culinary journey began when I embarked on a trip around Europe at the ripe old age of 21. My first stop was the heathery, tartan land of bonny Scotland...an interesting first choice when you can't speak English! My first job was as a 'meeter and greeter' in the Edinburgh restaurant Indigo Yard. Big Spanish smiles balanced my broken English and I made an effort to learn quickly. I had been itching to get in the kitchen and roll up my sleeves and my lucky break came one afternoon when the head chef, Colin, needed a hand. He called me into the kitchen and asked me to prepare the staff meal. With one chance to prove myself, I cooked a paella—mentally recalling the images and instructions passed down from my mother and grandmother. I rallied to conjure the best paella I could and while it perhaps was not my finest, Colin was sufficiently impressed with its flavours and my ability to offer me an apprenticeship. A generous guy, he took me under his wing and taught me a thing or two.

I started in the larder section preparing vegetables and quickly moved up to the fish section. Scotland, like Murcia, has an exciting array of fresh fish and crustaceans—salmon, kippers, oysters, langoustine and lobster to name but a few. I found myself preparing new and unusual things I hadn't encountered before. Hungry for knowledge, I soaked up every detail like a sponge. A year later, I continued to climb the ranks, heading the meat section, again learning and perfecting. From there I moved onward and upward to other sections, and then to other restaurants. For fear of sounding too buoyant at this point, I must mention the impressive list of

I'm proud to share my take on the food of my country.

burns and cuts I had acquired. I think every chef is on a continuous sharp and shiny learning curve, culminating in an all-important 'knife-reverence'. Only after a thousand band-aids, trimmed fingers and near misses do you really develop that essential, respectful relationship with the steely blade!

As well as culinary skills, I learned the importance of fitting into the kitchen environment and respectfully being a team player—no flying saucepans from me, only smiles!!

I met my beautiful wife Sascha while working at Indigo. She was the glamorous, blonde Australian waitress, and part of the reason I learnt English so quickly was so I could get to know her. The first meal I cooked her was a tortilla with homemade mayonnaise—simple and delicious—it was going to be a deal maker or breaker. I reckon is must have been a pretty good one, as she stuck around!

Like all good Spanish boys, I took her back to Spain to meet the family. This is when she began to understand how my passion for food was born.

From one continent to another, we left my hometown and headed south to Sascha's Australia. A country also blessed with glorious weather and fabulous food, this was my first foray into fine dining. I started working at the iconic Bel Mondo restaurant, nestled in the heart of Sydney's Rocks area, with spectacular views of the harbour bridge and opera house. Here I developed my knowledge and fascination with food presentation, something in which Bel Mondo excels. From there I moved next door to Cru, another world-class establishment. Celebrity chef Ed Hamalgyi employed me as chef de parti and, with diligent guidance, taught me a myriad of new skills. From there I followed Ed, as sous chef, to the Beach Road restaurant in stunning Palm Beach, with its tropical elegance and azure water views.

As if things couldn't get better, I moved on to work for Serge Dansereau at Bathers

Pavilion. An avid promoter of Australian produce, his menus are a festival of the very best of Aussie fruits, vegetables, dairy, meat and seafood. Under Serge, I also met two other chefs who would play an important part in my life. The first was Josh Gadsden, my great friend. A tenacious quick learner, he was an excellent team player and we somehow still managed to have a lot of fun in that fast-paced, stressful environment. The second was Stephane Jedgat, the very talented and superhuman pastry chef who started his day at 4am, worked his magic, then finished at 12am after producing a plethora of fine desserts and sweet miracles. He is no longer with us and is one of my best friends who I will miss every day forever.

Around this time, I met my agent Justine May, who put me forward for *Boys Weekend*, a new TV series with Manu Feildel, Gary Mehigan and Adrian Richardson. The show took us on adventures to unique locations in Australia, where we shopped for local delicacies and cooked up a storm—does it really get any better? We had way too much fun, cooked and ate some fabulous food and formed great friendships.

This meeting of minds led Manu Feildel to offer me the chance of a lifetime— working with him at Bilsons. Manu was head chef and under his direction the restaurant would ultimately earn an esteemed 3-hat award. More training and hard work under Manu's generous direction led me to my role as head chef at Bilsons Number One Wine Bar. His constant presence and sage advice taught me the most essential trait of a good head chef...always being in control. He deserves a special mention as I consider him my mentor and one of my brothers.

A calling back to my roots took me back to Spain to meet with the man who has been called the world's greatest chef, Ferran Adria at El Bulli. He will certainly have a place in the culinary history books for his molecular gastronomy. The restaurant is in the small town of Roses on the coast of Catalonia and has 3 Michelin stars and a two-year waiting list. There I learned to conjure delights such as the Deconstructed Spanish Omelette and Wild Rice Popcorn which I hope you will enjoy preparing as much as I did learning. With even more new-found skills and a mountain of inspiration, the time had come for me to take the risk, step into the abyss and open my own restaurant. I didn't have to think too long or too hard about which direction this would go—a real Tapas Chiringuito, showcasing the very best of Spanish tapas in a cool, fun, relaxed environment. I headed back to Australia.

Australia's laid-back lifestyle is perfect for tapas style eating. Aussies have embraced the unhurried, sharing ethos of eating a variety of small dishes punctuated with the odd cerveza. So much choice, so many options, half the fun is deciding on which little dishes will make up your meal. It is a style of eating that perfectly suits a romantic dinner for two, a relaxed lunch for six or a family dinner for ten.

It is Australia's largest tapas bar and you cannot run a vibrant, happy restaurant with excellent food on your own. So, I gathered a talented, enthusiastic, fabulous bunch of people, who make its day-to-day running an absolute joy. I run a tight ship with a happy crew and it makes me proud, every day, to be able to share my take on the food of my country. With their help we serve hundreds of paellas a day, made with fragrant saffron, smoky paprika and authentic Calasparra rice. A specially imported paella cooker helps us to produce the all important, perfect toasty soccarat crust...my mother is proud.

With the ocean on the doorstep we have access to the best seafood Australia has to offer. This makes cooking the perfect Tigers (Mussels with Romesco Sauce), Kingfish Ceviche or Garlic Prawns a breeze.

A liberal dose of flamenco music and the sound of lapping waves, washed down with a terracotta jug of sangria (my grandmother's recipe, of course), seems to leave people smiling and, even better, returning.

When the opportunity arose to write this book and share a little of El Toro Loco and my passion for beautiful food, it was a dream come true. How far I have come and how lucky I am to be able to do this. The Spanish people love their food dearly and these recipes are a collection of my favourites. With a head full of food, I was spoilt for choice as to which recipes to include. Despite this, I indulged and used it as an opportunity to sit down with my mother, grandmother, father, aunts and uncles, getting them to reminisce about their most poignant culinary memories and the aromas and tastes these evoked.

One thing is for sure, none of this would have been possible without my friends, family and wife. My mother and I, to this day have an extraordinary connection, while my eternally optimistic, hardworking father is my ultimate role model.

My beautiful, clever, giving wife Sascha, is my rock. Our wedding day in January 2010 was a festival of food and love. How often do you get given four legs of prized Iberico ham as a wedding present (thank you Eddie)? I sat down with my old friend Stephane the pastry chef and asked him to make Sascha the most decadent chocolate wedding cake he could come up with. He thought for only a second, before announcing it could only be his mother's dark, rich recipe laced with brandy. Sascha loved it and every guest became an instant chocoholic.

A naturally positive, cheery person she supports and motivates me every day, while still running our family and continuing her successful career. Every Sunday morning, I make fresh golden churros and thick hot chocolate and we sit in the garden chatting about our week. She makes me a better person and has been instrumental in helping me forge forward and advance in every way.

On arriving on Australian shores, Sascha's family welcomed me with open arms and have continued to be gracious and kind beyond expectation. In the absence of my own family, I cannot even begin to describe how grateful I am to them.

I am a passionate man and think honesty, respect and love go a long way to creating success. I apply them to my personal and working relationships, and to my cooking. Eating and cooking is at once pleasurable, celebratory and nurturing. Food cooked with love and passion tastes better than that cooked without—so why do it any other way?

I am honoured to share my recipes and memories with you: simple food from the bottom of my heart...tapas Maestre-style. Nothing but love and garlic...and a little chilli for those spicy moments.

Disfruta

BREAKFAST

The Virgin of la Fuensanta is the patron saint of Murcia. Legend says that in 1694, after a period of drought, she answered the prayers of the people for rain. Twice a year, starting at daybreak, a procession takes place through the streets in her honour. This early hour is when churros come into their own—sweet and crunchy they are a great way to kickstart the day.

There are many little shops in Murcia solely devoted to churros—all served with the obligatory thick hot chocolate. This is my recipe which I have been working on for nearly half a decade—light and crisp on the outside with an almost custard-like centre. We sell over 300 servings a week in the restaurant which is hopefully testament to the recipe. Enjoy!

CHURROS WITH CHOCOLATE

Serves: 4–6
Prep time: 10 minutes
Cooking time: 30 minutes

250ml (8fl oz) milk
1 teaspoon caster sugar
100g (3½oz) unsalted butter, chopped
2 vanilla beans, split, seeds scraped out
115g (4oz) plain flour
3 egg yolks
vegetable oil, for deep frying
caster sugar, to dust

CHOCOLATE SAUCE
250ml (8fl oz) condensed milk
200g (7oz) dark eating chocolate, chopped
splash milk
splash rum

To make chocolate sauce, stir condensed milk in a small saucepan, over medium heat until hot. Add chocolate. Whisk until smooth. Whisk in milk and rum. Remove from heat. Cover to keep warm.

Bring milk, sugar, butter and vanilla beans and seeds to a boil in a medium saucepan.

Discard vanilla beans. Remove from heat.

Sift in flour. Stir with a wooden spoon until combined and dough comes away from side of pan. Remove from heat. Stand, covered with plastic wrap, for 10 minutes.

Beat in egg yolks with wooden spoon, one at a time.

Spoon dough into a piping bag fitted with a 2cm (¾in) star nozzle.

Heat oil to 180°C (350°F) (when a cube of bread turns golden brown, oil is hot enough). Pipe 5cm (2in) lengths into oil, cutting off the dough with a sharp knife.

Deep fry churros until golden brown. Drain on absorbent paper.

Dust with caster sugar. Serve with chocolate sauce, custard or cream anglaise (see Basics & Sauces).

Tips: The amount of milk and rum you add to the sauce depends on whether you prefer a thick or thin sauce. Personally, I like a really thick sauce. - Save the vanilla beans—wash them and put them in sugar to infuse—making vanilla sugar.

It's not until you're asked to translate things that you sometimes realise how funny names and expressions that you use every day really are. Hence, telling you that this fluffy sponge roll, oozing with silky ganache and whipped cream, translates as the 'Gypsy's Arm', seems quite ridiculous! What isn't ridiculous is quite how decadent and delicious it is!

Brazo Gitano con Crema de Chocolate Blanco

GYPSY'S ARMS WITH WHITE CHOCOLATE CREAM

Serves: 4–6
Prep time: 30 minutes
Cooking time: 20 minutes

1 tablespoon cocoa powder
90g (3oz) flour
25g (1½ tablespoons) dark chocolate, grated
25g (1½ tablespoons) white chocolate, grated
3 eggs
115g (4oz) caster sugar
2 tablespoons boiling water

FILLING
100g (3½oz) white eating chocolate, chopped
250ml (8fl oz) pure or whipping cream
15ml (½fl oz) sherry Pedro Ximenez

Preheat oven to 200°C (400°F).

Grease a 25cm x 30cm (10in x 12in) Swiss roll pan. Line base with baking paper, extending paper 5cm (2in) over long sides of pan.

Sift cocoa and half the flour into a small bowl. Stir in the grated dark chocolate. Sift remaining flour into another bowl. Stir in the grated white chocolate.

Whisk eggs and sugar in a heatproof bowl over a saucepan of simmering water until thick and creamy. Divide mixture between flour mixtures. Stir to combine. Stir a tablespoon of boiling water into each to soften. Spoon alternate spoonfuls of mixture over base of prepared pan. Swirl with a knife to create a marbled effect.

Cook in the oven for about 15 minutes or until firm. Place a damp tea towel on the bench. Top with a sheet of baking paper. Immediately turn cake onto paper. Remove lining paper. Using a serrated knife, trim short edges of cake. Roll cake firmly from short side with baking paper inside. Cover with damp tea towel and cool.

Meanwhile, to make filling, place chocolate in a small bowl. Heat 125ml (4fl oz) of the cream in a small saucepan until hot. Pour over chocolate. Stir until smooth.

Beat sherry and remaining cream in small bowl of electric mixer until firm peaks form. Fold quarter of the cream mixture into white chocolate mixture to loosen. Fold in remaining cream mixture.

Unroll sponge. Spread with cream mixture. Roll up cake again, using paper as a guide. Wrap in plastic wrap. Refrigerate for 1 hour before serving.

Unwrap and slice with bread knife.

You can also serve this with Vanilla Custard or Cream Anglaise (see Basics & Sauces).

How to have potato, eggs and sausage at the same time for breakfast, Huevos Crujientes, a Spanish touch in every home.

Huevos Crujientes con Chorizo

CRISPY POTATO AND CHORIZO EGG

Serves: 2
Prep time: 5 minutes
Cooking time: 5 minutes

2 teaspoons olive oil
1 small potato, grated
1 small chorizo, cut into small dice (approximately 30g/1oz)
2 large eggs
1 teaspoon parsley, finely chopped
sourdough bread and lemon wedges, to serve

Heat oil in a non-stick frying pan.

Spoon potato into two greased large rings (12cm/4½in). Top with chorizo.

Cook until potato is crisp.

Crack eggs on top of mixture. Sprinkle with parsley. Cook until egg is just set.

Run a sharp knife around inside of rings to remove.

Serve Huevos Crujientes with bread and lemon wedges.

This is breakfast tapas style! My grandmother made this vibrant dish with fresh tomatoes from her garden—they were so big, we could fit three eggs in each one. Have lots of freshly baked bread on hand to mop up the mouthwatering juices.

Huevos a la Flamenca

FLAMENCA EGGS

Serves: 4
Prep time: 10 minutes
Cooking time: 15 minutes

4 large oxheart tomatoes (the
    size of your fist)
1 tablespoon olive oil
1 chilli, deseeded, chopped
2 garlic cloves, finely chopped
300ml (10fl oz) tomato juice
salt and pepper
4 large eggs
2 slices jamon Serrano, torn
2 tablespoons grated
    manchego cheese
sourdough bread, to serve

TOMATO SALAD

1 punnet yellow teardrop
    tomatoes, halved
1 punnet cherry tomatoes,
    halved
1 black Russian tomato,
    quartered
1 pink lady tomato, quartered
¼ bunch mint, leaves picked
¼ bunch basil, leaves picked
1 tablespoon olive oil

Preheat oven to 180°C (350°F).

Cut tops off tomatoes and slice the bottom off the tomato to stop the tomato from tipping over. Scoop out and discard pulp and seeds. Place tomato shells on an oven tray lined with baking paper.

Heat oil in a medium saucepan. Cook chilli and garlic until soft. Stir in tomato juice. Cook for about 5 minutes or until thickened. Season. Put in jug for easy pour.

Spoon hot mixture into tomato shells leaving room for the eggs. Crack an egg into each one. Replace tomato tops.

Cook in the oven for about 15 minutes or until tomato is tender and egg is set. Remove tops. Sprinkle with jamon and cheese.

Meanwhile, to make tomato salad, combine all ingredients in a large bowl. Season.

Arrange salad over serving plates. Top with baked tomato. Serve with sourdough to dip in tomato.

To dress the salad, use Lemon Vinaigrette (see Basics & Sauces).

Tip: You can use any type, size and colour tomatoes for the tomato salad—use whatever is fresh and in season.

I grew up in
Murcia, an area rich
in culinary tradition.

THE BARBECUE TOUCH ALLOWS THE SUGARS IN THE MELON TO CARAMELISE. PERFECT AS AN APPETISER TAPAS BEFORE A BIG MEAL.

Melon con Jamon Iberico

CARAMELISED MELON AND CRISPY JAMON IBERICO

Serves: 4
Prep time: 5 minutes
Cooking time: 10 minutes

½ rockmelon or honeydew
  melon, seeded
12 slices jamon Iberico
olive oil
fig vincoto

Cut melon into six wedges. Remove skin.

Wrap melon wedges in jamon, making sure all of the melon is covered.

Brush wedges with olive oil. Cook on a hot barbecue, drizzling with a little fig vincoto, until lightly browned.

TIP: FIG VINCOTO IS A SWEET, RICH VINEGAR AVAILABLE FROM DELICATESSENS. IF UNAVAILABLE, YOU CAN USE A BALSAMIC REDUCTION: SIMMER 250ML (8FL OZ) BALSAMIC VINEGAR UNTIL REDUCED BY HALF.

Tapas

...ca con aceite de oliva virgen org...

...organic extra virgin olive oil 'La Amaril...

..., manzanillas marinadas ala Murc...

...marinated manzanilla olives Murcian...

...itas con mayonesa

...ips, mayonnaise

My grandma makes it almost raw and runny inside, my mum cooks it all the way through and my dad likes it half and half! Every single Spaniard likes it a different way, but we all agree that life wouldn't be complete without this Spanish staple. Sit a slice in a big fresh bread roll and slather with lots of ajo (aioli) and salt. Perfect for breakfast or afternoon tea.

Tortilla de Patata

SPANISH POTATO OMELETTE

Serves: 4–6
Prep time: 5 minutes
Cooking time: 15 minutes

5 eggs
60ml (2fl oz) olive oil
1 large potato, cut into
  1cm (½in) slices
3 small onions, thinly sliced
3 garlic cloves, thinly sliced
salt and pepper
Aioli, see Basics & Sauces
lemon wedges

Break eggs into a medium-sized bowl. Whisk lightly to just break yolks.

Heat oil in a 20cm (8in) medium-sized non-stick frying pan.

Add potato, onion and garlic. Cook, over a medium heat, turning occasionally, until potato is tender and onion is soft, and remove from heat. Strain oil and stir mixture into eggs. Season.

Increase heat. Return mixture to frying pan when smokey hot.

Cook on one side for about 4 minutes on low heat or until just set. Invert tortilla onto a plate then slide it back into pan. Cook for a further 4 minutes.

Serve tortilla with Aioli (see Basics & Sauces) and lemon wedges.

A MODERN TAKE ON AN OLD CLASSIC THAT YOUNG AND OLD WILL ALL LOVE. THIS IS JUST A LOT OF FUN AND A VERY SIMPLE RECIPE! YOU CAN USE YOUR FAVOURITE FLAVOUR OF CHIPS AND TURN IT INTO YOUR OWN SIGNATURE SPANISH TREAT. *EN CINCO MINUTOS.*

5-MINUTE SPANISH POTATO OMELETTE

Serves: 2 in 13cm (5in) pans
Prep time: 5 minutes
Cooking time: 10 minutes

4 eggs
½ x 185g (6oz) bag of lime and
  black pepper flavoured
  potato chips
2 teaspoons olive oil
Aioli, see Basics & Sauces
1 teaspoon finely chopped
  parsley

Place eggs in a medium-sized bowl. Whisk lightly to just break yolks.

Place chips in a medium-sized bowl. Lightly crush. Add half the eggs. Stand for 2 minutes. Add remaining eggs.

Heat oil in a medium-sized non-stick frying pan. Add egg mixture.

Cook on one side for about 5 minutes or until just set. Invert tortilla onto a plate then slide it back into pan. Cook for a further 4 minutes.

Serve with Aioli (see Basics & Sauces) and chopped parsley.

TIP: USE ANY FLAVOUR OF POTATO CHIPS YOU LIKE.

For breakfast or afternoon tea, Tortilla de Patatas is a Spanish staple.

RUSTIC ZUCCHINI ROAST

Serves: 6–8
Prep time: 10 minutes
Cooking time: 40 minutes

80ml (2¾fl oz) extra virgin
    olive oil
4 garlic cloves, crushed
1kg (2lb) onions, thinly sliced
2kg (4lb) zucchini, thinly sliced
1 pinch ground white pepper
1 pinch sea salt
1 bunch oregano, leaves only
4 eggs, lightly beaten

Preheat oven to 170°C (300°F).

Heat oil in a large saucepan.

Add garlic. Cook on low heat, stirring for 1 minute, but do not allow to colour. Add onions. Cook, covered, stirring occasionally, for about 20 minutes or until soft.

Add zucchini. Cook, covered, stirring occasionally, for 30 minutes. Season with white pepper and salt to taste. Stir in oregano.

Place mixture in a preheated ovenproof serving dish. Stir through eggs. Flash in the oven for 15 minutes.

Season.

Tortillon Colientre de Jamon y Queso

MANCHEGO BREAD ROLLS

Serves: 6–8
Prep time: 5 minutes
Cooking time: 15 minutes

250ml (8fl oz) milk
250ml (8fl oz) water
100ml (3½fl oz) extra virgin
   olive oil
700g (24½ oz) tapioca flour
2 egg yolks
1 teaspoons hot paprika
1 tablespoon salt
400g (13oz) manchego cheese,
   grated
½ bunch parsley, chopped
   finely
100g (3½oz) Serrano jamon,
   chopped finely

Preheat oven to 200°C (400°F). Line an oven tray with baking paper.

Place milk, water and oil in a small saucepan. Bring to a boil. Remove from heat.

Place remaining ingredients in large bowl of an electric mixer with a dough hook attachment. Add milk mixture. Mix until mixture forms a soft dough.

Roll dough into 50g (1¾) balls. Place on prepared tray.

Cook in the oven for about 15 minutes or until golden and crisp.

Serve hot so the cheese is still melting.

You can serve these with Romesco Marinade as a dip (see Basics & Sauces).

MORNING TEA

Sardinas Crujientes con Judías Verdes y Chorizo

CALASPARRA RICE-CRUSTED SARDINES WITH GREEN BEANS AND CHORIZO

A LITTLE BITE OF THE MEDITERRANEAN IN EVERY MOUTHFUL—FRESH SARDINES WITH A DELICATE CRISP COATING BALANCED WITH SWEET GREEN BEANS AND A SPICY KICK FROM THE CHORIZO. A JOURNEY OF TEXTURE AND FLAVOUR THAT IS GUARANTEED TO EXCITE YOUR TASTEBUDS.

Serves: 2
Prep time: 10 minutes
Cook time: 10 minutes

50g (1¾oz) Calasparra rice
25g (⁴/₅oz) plain flour
2 tablespoons water
salt and pepper

6 butterflied sardines
1 tablespoon olive oil
50g (1¾oz) chorizo sausage, diced
100g (3½oz) green beans, thinly sliced

½ bunch parsley, finely chopped
2 garlic cloves, chopped
lemon wedges, to serve

Using a small grinder or mortar and pestle, grind rice to a coarse powder. Place on a plate.

Whisk flour and water in small bowl to form a smooth batter. Season.

Pat sardines dry with absorbent paper. Dip skin-side only in batter, then dip both sides into powdered rice.

Heat oil in a non-stick frying pan.

Cook the sardines on medium heat, skin-side down, for about 4 minutes or until crust is crisp and golden. Turn and cook for about a further 30 seconds. Drain on absorbent paper.

Add chorizo to same clean pan. Cook, over medium heat, stirring occasionally, until lightly browned. Add beans. Cook, stirring occasionally, for about 5 minutes or until tender. Stir in parsley and garlic. Season to taste.

Place bean and chorizo mixture on serving plate. Top with sardines. Serve with lemon wedges.

TIP: IF GRINDING RICE IN A MORTAR AND PESTLE, GRIND ONLY A LITTLE AT A TIME. IF YOU ADD ALL THE RICE IN ONE GO, IT WILL BE IMPOSSIBLE TO CRUSH. MAKE SURE IT IS ALMOST POWDER, NOT COARSE.
YOU CAN ALSO USE GRILLED SARDINES FOR THIS RECIPE (SEE BASICS & SAUCES).

A little bite of the Mediterranean in every mouthful.

VISUALLY STUNNING, THIS IS ANOTHER SIGNATURE DISH IN MY RESTAURANT AND POSSIBLY THE BEST SELLER. IT'S A PARTY FOR THE TASTEBUDS—A REFRESHING COMBINATION OF SWEETNESS, ACIDITY AND SPICE. ITS CROWNING GLORY IS A SHOT OF TIGRES MILK (THE MILKY JUICE FROM THE CEVICHE) AND VODKA.

THIS RECIPE IS INSPIRED BY MY VERY GOOD FRIEND AND THE BEST PERUVIAN CHEF IN THE WORLD DIEGO MUÑOZ.

KINGFISH CEVICHE

Serves: 2
Prep time: 15 minutes
Cooking time: 10 minutes

1 tablespoon olive oil
1 small stick celery
1 fresh long red chilli
1 garlic clove
1cm (½in) piece fresh ginger
½ bunch coriander
juice of 2 lemons
juice of 1 lime
200g (7oz) sashimi grade
    kingfish fillet, cut into 1cm
    (½in) dice
½ Spanish onion, thinly sliced
1 ice cube
2 shots of vodka

POACHED SWEET POTATO

200ml Sugar Syrup (see Basics
    & Sauces)
1 star anise
1 sweet potato (250g/8oz),
    peeled, cut into 1cm (½in)
    dice
juice of 1 lime

To make poached sweet potato, stir water, sugar and star anise in a small saucepan, over low heat, until sugar is dissolved. Add potato. Boil gently until potato is just tender. Drain. Place in a bowl. Drizzle with lime juice.

Meanwhile, place oil, celery, chilli, garlic, ginger, coriander and the lemon and lime juice in a small processor. Process until smooth. Place in a serving bowl. Add fish, onion and ice cube. Stand for 4 minutes—this allows the acid from the citrus juice to cook the protein in the fish.

Place a shot of vodka in each shot glass. Add a splash of the cloudy citrus juice from the fish.

Serve ceviche with sweet potato and vodka shot.

TIP: IF KINGFISH IS NOT AVAILABLE, YOU CAN USE ATLANTIC SALMON OR TUNA.

I AM FASCINATED BY THE QUALITIES OF SOFT SHELL CRAB AND REMEMBER THE FIRST TIME I TRIED IT IN A LITTLE CHINESE RESTAURANT. IT IS BRILLIANT FOR FRYING, BECOMING CRISP AND SWEET. HAVING GIVEN IT A SPANISH TWIST, IT IS NOW ONE OF MY FAVOURITE TAPAS.

SOFT SHELL CRAB AND SAUTÉ OF EDAMAME

Serves: 2
Prep time: 10 minutes
Cooking time: 5 minutes

500g (1lb) frozen edamame beans
1 chorizo sausage, chopped
1 garlic clove, finely chopped
1 bunch chives, chopped
juice of 1 lime
2 tablespoons preserved lemon, sliced julienne (available from the deli)

DEEP FRIED CRAB
200g (7oz) rice flour
2 teaspoons chilli powder
2 pinch of Szechwan pepper
2 teaspoon hot paprika
2 teaspoon sea salt
4 soft shell crabs, cleaned, quartered
vegetable oil, for deep frying

Place edamame beans in a small bowl. Cover with water. Stand 5 minutes. Drain. Remove beans from shell. Discard shell.

Heat a large saucepan. Add chorizo. Cook, over medium heat, until fat starts to break down. Add garlic, chives and beans. Sauté, stirring occasionally, until beans are tender. Stir in lime juice and preserved lemon.

To prepare crab, combine flour, chilli powder, Szechwan pepper, paprika and salt in a shallow bowl.

Dust crab portions in flour mixture. Deep fry until golden. Drain on absorbent paper.

Serve crab with edamame sauté.

TIP: IF YOU DON'T HAVE EDAMAME YOU COULD USE FAVA BEANS OR FRESH PEAS INSTEAD.

Crab with a Spanish twist is one of my favourite tapas.

More genius inspiration inspired from world class El Bulli chef Ferran Adria. Fast, classy and absolutely delicious. Suquet is the name of the sauce in Catalan. Thanks Ferran for your inspiration.

Carpaccio de atun con Tomato Suquet

TUNA CARPACCIO WITH TOMATO SAUCE

Serves: 2
Prep time: 5 minutes
Cooking time: 10 minutes

1 large potato
1 tablespoon olive oil
3 garlic cloves, chopped
½ bunch parsley, chopped
1 tomato, chopped
½ teaspoon smoked paprika
250ml (8fl oz) fish stock
1 tablespoon aioli (see Basics
& Sauces)
salt and pepper
300g (10oz) sashimi grade
tuna, sliced very thinly

Cut potato in half lengthways. Scoop out balls using a Parisian scoop (melon baller).

Heat oil in a small frying pan. Add potato balls. Cook, stirring, until golden brown.

Add garlic, parsley, tomato and paprika. Cook, stirring, for 3 minutes. Stir in stock. Simmer until potatoes are tender. Stir in aioli. Season.

Arrange tuna, in a single layer, on a serving platter.

Cover the tuna with the hot suquet (sauce).

Tip: If tuna isn't available you can use kingfish or salmon instead.

My favourite treat as a kid and to be honest I can't believe this is one of the biggest sellers in my restaurant—so creamy! It is also a very smart way to get your children to eat seafood. I can't wait to make it for my children.

BECHAMEL SAUCE AND PRAWN-STUFFED MUSSELS

Serves: 2–3
Prep time: 30 minutes
Cooking time: 30 minutes

ROMESCO SAUCE

3 piquillo peppers
1 garlic clove
½ bunch coriander
1 chilli
10 almonds, toasted
1 tablespoon extra virgin olive oil
squeeze of lemon

WHITE SAUCE

10g butter
2 teaspoons plain flour
100ml (3½fl oz) milk
pinch white pepper

TIGERS

100ml (3½fl oz) white wine
10 large black mussels
4 large prawns, peeled, cooked and
   chopped
2 piquillo peppers, finely chopped
1 tablespoon finely chopped parsley
1 garlic clove, finely chopped
1 pink eschallot, finely chopped
extra flour, for dusting
2 eggs, beaten lightly
50g (1¾oz) panko
olive oil, to shallow fry

To make romesco sauce, blend or process all ingredients until smooth.

To make white sauce, melt butter in a small saucepan. Add flour. Cook, stirring, until mixture bubbles. Gradually whisk in milk. Cook, stirring, until white sauce boils and thickens. Season with white pepper.

To prepare Tigers, bring wine to boil in a medium saucepan. Add mussels. Cook, covered, for a few minutes until mussels open. Remove from heat.

Remove mussel meat from shells and roughly chop. Reserve ten half-shells.

Add mussel meat to white sauce, with prawns, peppers, parsley, garlic and eschallot. Divide mixture among mussel shells.

Dust filled half shells with flour. Dip in egg then panko. Repeat crumbing twice.

Shallow fry until golden brown and crisp. Drain on absorbent paper. Serve with romesco coulis.

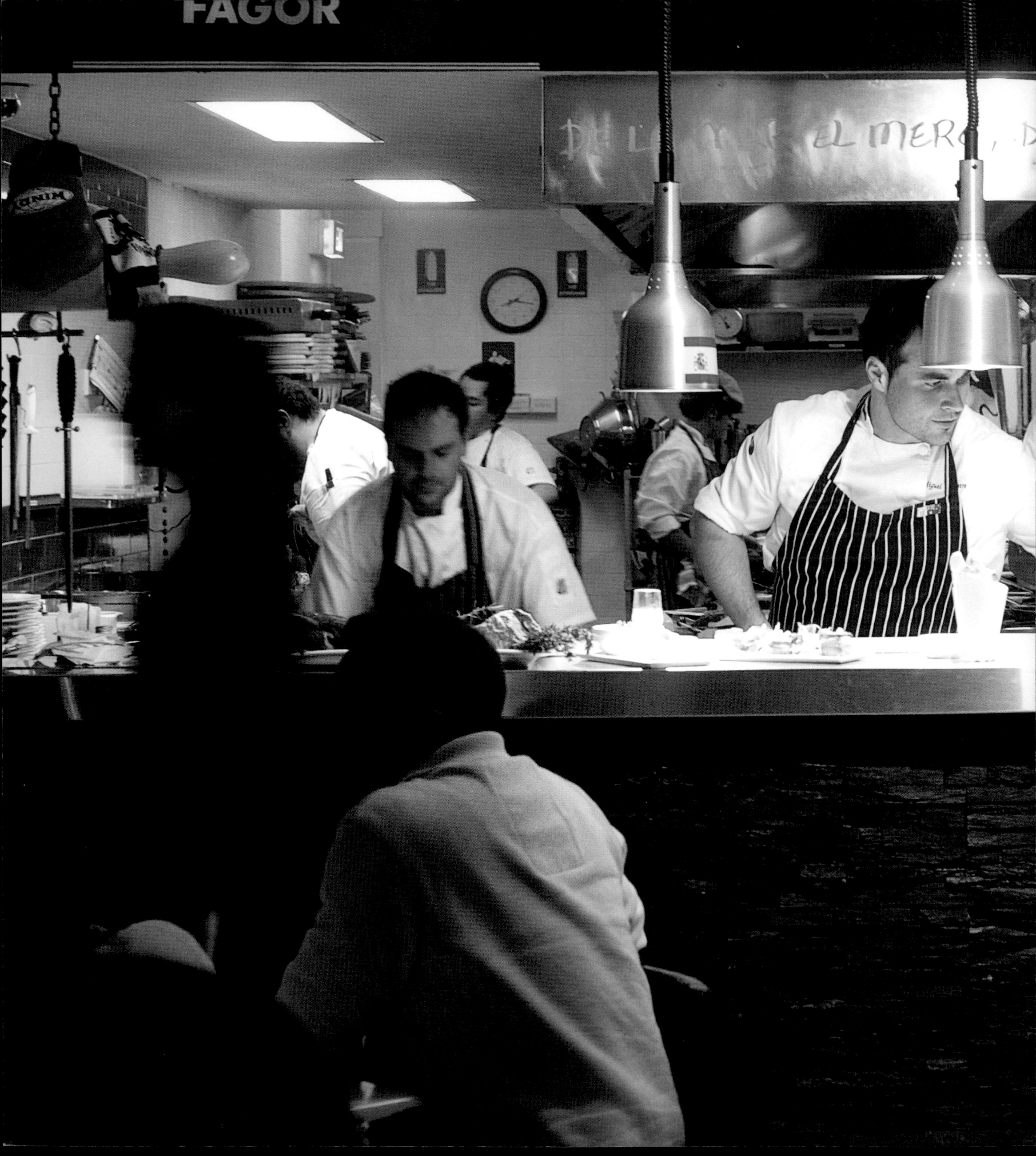
FAGOR

This is one of the most popular tapas in Spain—rich spicy sausage, zesty pickled eschallots and fresh apple cider. The secret is to make sure the pan is really hot before adding the cider—that way you will burn off the raw alcohol, leaving behind the wonderful deep apple flavours.

Chorizo a la Sidra

CHORIZO CIDER STYLE

Serves: 2
Prep time: 5 minutes
Cooking time: 10 minutes

4 pink eschallots, peeled
250ml (8fl oz) water
250ml (8fl oz) white wine vinegar
2 tablespoons caster sugar
2 chorizo sausage, thickly sliced
1 tablespoon finely chopped parsley
50ml (1¾fl oz) fresh apple cider
extra chopped parsley, to serve

For the pickling process, bring eschallots, water, vinegar and sugar to a boil in a small saucepan. Simmer until eschallots are soft. Drain.

Heat a small, heavy based frying pan until very hot. Cook chorizo for about 3 minutes or until golden brown. Stir in eschallot mixture and parsley. Add cider. Deglaze until almost evaporated.

Serve chorizo in a clay pot with extra parsley.

I HAVE EATEN GARLIC PRAWNS ALL OVER THE WORLD AND THE MOST COMMON MISTAKE PEOPLE MAKE IS OVER COMPLICATING WHAT IS ESSENTIALLY THE MARRIAGE OF THREE SIMPLE INGREDIENTS. FOR A WINNING DISH, FOLLOW MY RECIPE AND BE SURE TO USE EXTRA VIRGIN OLIVE OIL AND THE FRESHEST PRAWNS!

Gambas al Ajillo

GARLIC PRAWNS

Serves: 1
Prep time: 4 minutes
Cooking time: 3 minutes

50ml (1¾fl oz) extra virgin olive oil
4 large king prawns, peeled, de-veined
3 garlic cloves, chopped
½ bunch parsley, finely chopped
lemon wedges and fresh crusty bread, to serve

Heat oil in a small cast iron or clay dish.

Add prawns. Cook for about 3 minutes or until just cooked (they turn orange when cooked through). Stir in garlic and parsley.

Eat the prawns while still sizzling with a squeeze of lemon juice. Serve with bread to dip in the oil, which has been beautifully infused with flavours of the prawns, garlic and parsley.

TIP: BUY THE BEST PRAWNS FOR THIS DISH, IT WILL BE WORTH IT.

Hot Spanish days call
for cool food with
minimal preparation.

THE SPANISH SUMMER BRINGS SOME LONG, HOT SIZZLING DAYS, WHICH CALL FOR COOL FOOD AND MINIMAL PREPARATION. THIS ALL POINTS TO ONE THING...GAZPACHO! LIGHT AND REFRESHING, IT'S JAM PACKED WITH SUMMER ZING.

GAZPACHO FROM ANDALUCIA

Serves: 4
Prep time: 20 minutes

1 red capsicum, deseeded,
   chopped
1 yellow capsicum, deseeded,
   chopped
1 green capsicum, deseeded,
   chopped
4 large truss tomatoes,
   chopped
2 garlic cloves
½ bulb fennel, chopped
1 jalapeno pepper
1 large cucumber, chopped
2 black anchovies
2 white anchovies
½ bunch coriander
½ bunch parsley
½ bunch basil
400ml (13½ fl oz) extra virgin
   olive oil
ice cubes, to serve
4 slices jamon Iberico, to
   garnish

To make gazpacho, place all ingredients, except ice and jamon, in a food processor. Process until smooth (you can do this in batches if your processor is not big enough).

Strain through a sieve.

Serve gazpacho in a chilled cocktail glass with ice cubes. Garnish with jamon.

TIP: BLACK ANCHOVIES ARE SOLD IN TINS AND JARS AND HAVE BEEN PRESERVED IN OIL. WHITE ANCHOVIES ARE FRESH ANCHOVIES WHICH HAVE BEEN MARINATED IN VINEGAR—THEY ARE AVAILABLE FROM DELICATESSENS.

PUT LEFTOVER GAZPACHO INTO ICE-CUBE TRAYS AND FREEZE SO YOU CAN USE IT FRESH NEXT TIME.

THIS IS A GREAT DISH FOR SUMMER—A BEAUTIFUL COMBINATION OF FRESH VEGETABLES FROM YOUR GARDEN. NORMALLY SERVED AS A CHILLED SALAD, BUT WHEN IT IS SERVED HOT, A BREAST OF CHICKEN OR GRILLED MEAT MAKE GOOD ACCOMPANIMENTS.

SPANISH RATATOUILLE

Serves: 6–8
Prep time: 30 minutes
Cooking time: 45 minutes

2 large zucchini
2 baby squash
2 red onions
1 large eggplant
2 red capsicum
2 green capsicum
2 yellow capsicum
olive oil, for frying
10 garlic cloves
2 hot chillies, seeded
1 bunch thyme
1 bunch parsley
1 bunch oregano, leaves only
1 bunch chives
1 tablespoon sherry vinegar
juice of 1 lemon
salt and pepper

Cut all vegetables into small dice.

Heat a little oil in a large, deep, frying pan. Add zucchini. Cook, stirring, until, golden brown. Transfer to a large bowl. Repeat with remaining vegetables, frying separately and adding more oil as necessary.

Finely chop garlic, chillies and herbs. Add to vegetable mixture with vinegar and juice. Season.

Serve warm or cold.

TIP: PERFECT GARNISH FOR A LAMB DISH.

IF YOU SERVE THIS AS A SALAD, IT IS DELICIOUS DRESSED WITH A BLACK OLIVE VINAIGRETTE (SEE BASICS & SAUCES)..

WITH A HINT OF CHILLI, A WHIFF OF PAPRIKA AND A BITE OF SPICY SAUSAGE, MICHIRONES IS THE SPANISH VERSION OF BAKED BEANS. FILLING AND NUTRITIOUS, EAT THEM ON TOAST OR ALONE WITH MELTED MANCHEGO CHEESE FOR A QUICK SNACK OR THE PERFECT BREAKFAST.

Michirones

SPANISH BAKED BEANS

Serves: 4
Prep time: 5 minutes + 24 hours soaking time
Cooking time: 40 minutes

500g (1lb) dried lima beans
1L (32fl oz) chicken stock
1 dried chilli
1 garlic clove, chopped
1 chorizo sausage, sliced
75g (2½oz) jamon Serrano,
    cut in small cubes
1 bay leaf
1 teaspoon spicy paprika
1 teaspoon sweet paprika
1 pinch smoked paprika
lemon and lime rind, to
    garnish
grated Manchego cheese, to
    serve

Soak beans for 24 hours, changing the water every 8 hours. Drain.

Bring beans to boil in a large saucepan of boiling water (do not add salt as this can toughen the beans). Boil gently for 10 minutes. Drain.

Bring beans, stock, chilli, garlic, chorizo, jamon, bay leaf and paprikas to a boil. Simmer until beans are soft.

Serve beans in a large clay dish with some of the stock. Garnish with lemon and lime rind. Serve with cheese.

TIP: LIMA BEANS ARE ALSO REFERRED TO AS BUTTER BEANS. FOR A QUICK VERSION, USE 3 X 400G (13OZ) TINS OF BEANS, OMITTING THE FIRST TWO STEPS.

CROQUETTES MEAN ONE THING…ME STANDING ON A STOOL AS A LITTLE BOY, PERFORMING THE ALL-IMPORTANT TASK OF HELPING MUM DO THE CRUMBING. LAUGHING AND JOKING, WE WOULD HAVE QUITE A PRODUCTION LINE GOING. MY LITTLE HANDS DEVELOPED A SUPER SPEEDY TECHNIQUE AS I KNEW WHAT WAS AT THE END OF THE LINE—GOLDEN CRUNCHY ORBS WITH FLUFFY FISH AND POTATO CENTRES!

Croquetas de Bacalao de Mi Mama

BACALAO SALTED COD CROQUETTES

Serves: 4
Prep time: 35 minutes + overnight soaking
Cooking time: 1 hour

175g (6oz) bacalao (salt cod)
1 medium potato (200g/7oz)
1 tablespoon olive oil
5 garlic cloves, finely chopped
125ml (4fl oz) cream
5 sprigs thyme
finely grated rind of 1 lemon
splash of lemon juice
½ bunch chives, chopped
plain flour, for dusting
2 eggs, lightly beaten
200g (7oz) panko (Japanese breadcrumbs)
vegetable oil, for deep frying
aioli, to serve

Rinse salt from cod. Place in a medium-sized bowl, and cover with water. Refrigerate, covered, overnight, changing water every 6 hours. Drain. Cut into three pieces.

Preheat oven to 200°C (400°F). Bake potato for about 40 minutes or until tender. Cool slightly. Cut in half and scoop out centres into a saucepan. Mash until smooth. Cook, stirring, over a low heat, for 3 minutes to evaporate any moisture. Stir in oil and garlic. Remove from heat.

Meanwhile, bring cream and thyme to a boil in a small saucepan. Add fish. Simmer for about 8 minutes or until soft. Drain. Cool. Remove any skin and bones. Using your hands, shred finely.

Combine fish, potato, rind, juice and chives in a medium bowl.

Roll mixture into walnut-sized balls. Coat with flour, and dip in egg then panko. Dip in egg and panko a second time—this will give a lovely crisp coating. Deep fry balls until golden brown and hot.

Serve croquettes with aiolo or a white sauce with caperberries (see Basics & Sauces).

A FISHY TALE—'*MATRIMONIOS*' TRANSLATES AS 'WEDDING' IN SPANISH, AND THIS TAPA IS A UNION OF ANCHOVIES! ONE WHITE, PLUMP AND JUICY, PRESERVED IN WINE VINEGAR—THE OTHER SMALL AND SALTY WITH A ROBUST FLAVOUR KICK. WRAPPED AROUND A SWEET PICKLED ESCHALLOT, THEY CREATE THE ULTIMATE FLAVOUR EXPLOSION! THE THIRD THING IN THIS MARRIAGE? NOT THE MOTHER IN-LAW, BUT THE ESSENTIAL ICY COLD BEER.

WHITE AND BLACK ANCHOVY SKEWERS

Serves: 4
Prep time: 5 minutes
Cooking time: 5 minutes

10 small eschallots, peeled
250ml (8fl oz) water
60ml (2fl oz) white wine
   vinegar
75g (2½oz) caster sugar
10 white anchovies
   (boquerones)
10 black anchovies
10 skewers
chopped parsley and olive oil,
   to serve

Bring eschallots, water, vinegar and sugar to a boil in a small saucepan. Simmer until tender. Drain. Cool.

Lay white anchovies on a work surface. Top with black anchovies and an eschallot.

Roll up, keeping eschallot in middle. Thread onto a skewer.

Sprinkle with parsley and drizzle with olive oil.

LUNCH

Caldero Murciano

MARINARA STYLE RICE

This dish is named after the cast iron pot in which it is cooked, the 'caldero' or cauldron. The best Murcian restaurants have ancient specimens, passed down through generations, and the locals cook this dish on the beach, their old pots hung over an open fire. A good caldero is one that is older than you!

My mother's family used to own La Manga where the best caldero is made. She would prepare this rice in huge quantities for all our family gatherings. Other than the unique cooking pot, this dish also requires you to use mullet and ñoras (dried capsicums) —no substitutions here if you want to make the real deal.

This hearty dish is no light meal and it definitely requires a siesta when finished.

Serves: 4
Prep time: 25 minutes
Cooking time: 40 minutes

125ml (4fl oz) virgin olive oil
2 noras (small dried capsicum—
available from Spanish
delicatessens)
200g (7oz) fish heads (ask your
fishmonger for these)

2 ripe tomatoes, peeled, chopped
2L (64fl oz) water
2 garlic bulbs, cloves peeled
200g (7oz) mullet, thickly sliced
200g (7oz) trevalla, snapper or leather
jacket fillets, thickly sliced

200g (7oz) monk fish or deep sea
perch fillets, thickly sliced
400g (13oz) Calasparra rice
200g (7oz) king prawns

Preheat oven to 160°C (315°F).

Heat oil in a large cast iron pot until it is smoking hot. Cook ñoras for 1 minute. Remove with a slotted spoon. Set aside. Reduce heat.

To make the stock, add fish heads to same pot. Cook, stirring occasionally, for 5 minutes. Remove and discard. Add tomatoes. Cook, stirring, for 5 minutes. Stir in water. Bring to a simmer.

Using a mortar and pestle, crush one of the ñoras and half of the garlic to a smooth paste. Add mixture to pot. Simmer for 5 minutes. Add fish. Simmer for 5 minutes. Remove fish with a slotted spoon and place on an oven tray. Cover with foil and transfer to the oven to keep warm.

Remove and reserve 1 cup of the stock.

Add rice to remaining stock. Season. Simmer for about 20 minutes or until tender. Add prawns for last 2 minutes of cooking.

Meanwhile, place reserved stock and remaining noras and garlic in a processor. Process to combine.

To serve, place fish in a large serving bowl. Pour over garlic stock mixture. Serve with rice and Aioli (see Basics & Sauces).

THERE IS A LITTLE CORNER SHOP IN MY HOMETOWN THAT SELLS THIS FAVOURITE FOR 3 EUROS AND I CAN'T GET ENOUGH. IT IS A LITTLE POT OF LAYERED INDULGENCE—MELTINGLY TENDER EGGPLANT, PRAWNS, JAMON, CREAMY SAUCE AND GRUYERE CHEESE.

CREAMED AUBERGINE

Serves: 4
Prep time: 25 minutes
Cooking time: 35 minutes

125ml (4fl oz) olive oil
4 garlic cloves, thinly sliced
2 small eggplants (500g/1lb),
    cut into 2cm (¾in) slices
50g (1¾oz) plain flour
salt and pepper
12 prawns, peeled, de-veined
50g (1¾oz) thinly sliced jamon
    Serrano
1 small onion, finely chopped
50g (1¾oz) plain flour
250ml (8fl oz) milk
250ml (8fl oz) beef stock
50g (1¾oz) gruyere cheese,
    grated

Preheat oven to 180°C (350°F).

Heat 1 tablespoon of the oil in a frying pan. Add garlic. Cook over medium heat until soft. Remove and set aside.

Dust eggplant slices with flour and season. Heat 2 tablespoons of remaining oil in same hot pan. Add half the eggplant slices. Cook for about 5 minutes on each side or until golden brown and tender. Remove and drain on absorbent paper. Repeat with 2 tablespoons oil and remaining eggplant. Divide eggplant among four ovenproof ramekins (1¾ cup capacity). Top with prawns and jamon.

Heat remaining oil in a medium saucepan. Add onion. Cook, stirring occasionally, until soft and golden brown. Add flour. Cook, stirring, for 1 minute. Gradually whisk in milk and stock. Cook, whisking, until smooth and thickened. Season. Strain.

Divide sauce among ramekins. Sprinkle with cheese. Place ramekins on an oven tray.

Cook in the oven for about 20 minutes or until prawns are cooked and cheese is golden.

TIP: SEASON (BY ADDING SALT) TO THE EGGPLANT BEFORE COOKING—IT WILL RELEASE MORE FLAVOUR.

When i was a kid my grandmother took great delight in squeezing my pudgy cheeks and comparing them to those of a cute, chubby, suckling pig. Pig cheeks are a cheap cut and melt-in-the-mouth tender once braised. The sweet vanilla lifts the dish to culinary heights.

Mejillana de Jabalí a la Vainilla

VANILLA INFUSED WILD BOAR CHEEKS

Serves: 2
Prep time: 10 minutes
Cooking time: 2 hours

4 wild boar or pig cheeks, trimmed

1 sprig of thyme, leaves only

sea salt

1 tablespoon extra virgin olive oil

1 bulb garlic, cloves peeled and chopped

1 pink eschallot, finely chopped

1 onion, finely diced

1 carrot, finely diced

1 celery stick, finely diced

5 dried juniper berries

2 vanilla beans, split, seeds scraped out

500ml (17fl oz) beef stock

500ml (17fl oz) red wine (shiraz or merlot is best)

Place meat, thyme and salt in a bowl. Using your hands, rub salt and thyme into meat.

Heat half the oil in a medium saucepan until very hot. Add meat in batches. Cook until browned all over. Set aside.

Reduce heat. Add remaining oil to same pan. Add garlic, eschallot, onion, carrot, celery and berries. Cook, stirring occasionally, for about 10 minutes or until vegetables are soft.

Return meat to pan with vanilla beans and seeds, stock and wine. Bring to boil. Cover with a cartouche. Simmer, skimming fat from top every 30 minutes, for 1½–2 hours, or until meat is very tender.

Tip: 'Cartouche' is the French term for a piece of baking paper placed over food to keep in moisture during or after cooking. Cut a piece of paper larger than your pan. Fold in half, then in half again and again, and trim the outside edge to a curve so it's half the pan width. Open pleated circle and place into the pan to sit snugly over the top of your food while cooking.

THIS TAPA WAS CREATED ORIGINALLY FOR MY SOUS CHEF AND GOOD FRIEND RUBEN. WE USED TO ROAST SUCKLING PIGS EVERY FRIDAY AND IF THERE WAS ANY LEFT WE WOULD SHRED IT AND PUT IN A SALAD. IT WAS AN INSTANT HIT AT THE RESTAURANT SO WE DECIDED TO MODIFY IT SLIGHTLY AND ARE NOW USING THE BEST BIT OF THE PIG—PORK BELLY. IT'S ONE OF OUR HUGE SELLERS.

PORK SALAD

Serves: 2
Prep time: 30 minutes + resting time
Cooking time: 4 hours

200g (7oz) pork belly
1 star anise
1 cinamon quill
1 chilli, dried
3 dried porcinis
1 bay leaf
5 garlic cloves, sliced
800ml (27fl oz) beef stock

SALAD

½ carrot, shaved with
    mandolin
½ bulb fennel, shaved with
    mandolin
10 parsley leaves, picked and
    washed
10 mint leaves, picked and
    washed
10 coriander leaves, picked
    and washed
2 fresh chillies deseeded and
    julienned (on ice so they will
    curl like pig's tails!)

Season pork belly and leave out of fridge for 30 minutes to reach room temperature.

In a medium-sized saucepan, sauté for 5 minutes star anise, cinnamon, dried chilli, porcinis, bay leaf and garlic.

Add beef stock and bring to boil. Simmer for 10 minutes. Add pork belly to stock and simmer, covered, for 4 hours.

When cooked, press pork belly pieces between 2 trays with a little weight on top to become flat. Place in fridge overnight.

When the pork is nice and flat, cut in squares and pan fry (skin side down) for 10 minutes on low heat in a non-stick pan.

Dry the meat in oven with skin side up for 5 minutes at160°C (320°F), grill mode, until skin is crispy like crackling.

SALAD
Combine all ingredients in mixing bowl and dress with lemon vinaigrette (see Basics & Sauces). Season to taste.

To serve, set the salad on a plate with the pork belly squares.

A MURCIAN SALAD MUST OF COURSE HAVE THE BEST OF MURCIAN PRODUCE! FRESH, JUICY SUN-RIPENED TOMATOES, SHINY BLACK MANZANILLA OLIVES, CRISP WHITE ONIONS AND THE FRESHEST TUNA YOU CAN FIND. MY MUM USED TO PACK THESE INGREDIENTS INTO A HUGE FRENCH BAGUETTE FOR MY SCHOOL LUNCH—TALK ABOUT ENVIOUS CLASSMATES.

MURCIAN TUNA SALAD

Serves: 2
Prep time: 10 minutes
Cooking time: 1 minute

100g (3½oz) tuna loin, thickly
  sliced
2½ tablespoons extra virgin
  olive oil
salt and pepper
2 tablespoons sherry vinegar
4 very ripe heirloom or oxheart
  tomatoes, quartered
10 pitted black olives
  (manzanilla)
½ white onion, very thinly
  sliced
10 mint leaves
10 parsley leaves
10 tarragon leaves
10 caperberries
2 soft boiled eggs, quartered

Bring tuna to room temperature. Place in a bowl with 2 teaspoons of the oil. Toss to combine. Season.

Heat a grill pan until very hot. Cook tuna for 30 seconds on each side.

Whisk vinegar and remaining oil in a large bowl. Season. Add tomatoes, olives, onion, herbs and caperberries.

To assemble salad, divide tomato mixture over serving plates. Top with tuna and eggs.

You can also serve this salad with roasted garlic (see Basics & Sauces).

TIP: ALWAYS USE TOMATOES AT ROOM TEMPERATURE TO APPRECIATE THEIR FULL FLAVOUR.

PAELLA A LA MAESTRE

How do you define a whole country in just one dish? Paella! Brimming with seafood, served in its iconic pan and laced with saffron and paprika, it embodies the passion and spirit of the Spanish people.

The best paella uses the precious Calasparra or Bomba rice, proudly grown in my hometown of Murcia. A mountainous region, the rice is grown along the River Segura where a unique irrigation system allows it to mature slowly. This results in a drier grain that can absorb a third more of the flavoursome cooking stock than other rices, while still holding its shape.

Australia's seafood is among the world's best and it makes truly wonderful paella—Queensland prawns, Spring Bay mussels and freshwater yabbies are among my favourites. My old friend Frank at De Costi looks after me well. Establish a good relationship with your local fishmonger and you will always have a good paella.

This recipe has been in my family for three generations and is a unique and original interpretation of a classic. My personal touch is a shortcut which produces an intense flavour in less time—I make the sofrito with raw ingredients to preserve the flavour of the garlic and saffron. Frying the rice before adding the sofrito also results in a more even 'socarrada'—the prized golden crust which forms on the base of the pan.

My restaurant sells over 1000 paellas a week and Sydney's finest chefs, including Tetsuya Wakuda and Manu Feildel, have rated it as the city's best. A much-loved family recipe, it carries my mothers surname, Maestre, as its legacy. Cook and enjoy it with friends and family...and as we say in Spain, 'ole'!

Serves: 4–6
Prep time: 10 minutes
Cooking time: 30 minutes

1 tablespoon olive oil
400g (13oz) Calasparra rice
500g (1lb) mussels, cleaned
2 king prawns
1 blue swimmer crab, cleaned,
    quartered
4 baby calamari hoods, cleaned
4 yabbies
2L (64fl oz) fish or chicken stock
salt and pepper
200g (7oz) fresh or frozen peas

2 lemons, halved
2 limes, halved
chopped parsley, to garnish

SOFRITO
150ml (5fl oz) olive oil
3 teaspoons sherry vinegar
3 large ripe oxheart tomatoes
½ chorizo sausage—
3 pink eschallots, peeled
4 cloves garlic, peeled

4 piquillo peppers
½ bunch thyme, leaves only
½ bunch mint
½ bunch parsley
½ bunch coriander
1 bunch chives
1 teaspoon saffron threads
1 teaspoon sweet paprika
1 teaspoon spicy paprika
1 teaspoon smoked paprika

To make sofrito, place all ingredients in a food processor. Process until smooth. Set aside.

Heat oil in a large paella pan. Add rice. Cook, stirring occasionally, for about 5 minutes or until it changes from white to transparent.

Stir in 12 large tablespoons of the sofrito. Cook for 3 minutes. Add seafood and stock. Season. Cook, over medium heat, without stirring, for about 25 minutes or until stock has been absorbed and rice is almost tender. Reduce heat to low and cook for a further 3 minutes to form a nice 'soccarrada'. If hob plate is not as big as pan, move pan around a little during cooking to ensure even heat. Add peas and remove from heat.

Stand, covered with a tea towel, for 5 minutes. Squeeze over lemons and limes and season. Garnish with parsley. Serve paella warm, not steaming hot.

Tip: Never scrub a paella pan. Wash it carefully with hot water only.

RABBIT AND GARLIC RICE

Arroz y Conejo al Ajillo

Hunting rabbit at the end of summer to make this earthy dish is an adventure I always look forward to. Man against nature—you need cunning, patience and tenacity to outwit this clever little animal. A great alternative to chicken, wild rabbit is a lean meat bursting with flavour. It merits lots of garlic and earthy herbs—rosemary or sage can be used instead of marjoram and thyme if you prefer. Serve with aioli, fresh sourdough and a cheeky glass of Rioja.

Serves: 4
Prep time: 35 minutes + resting time
Cook time: 40 minutes

1 fresh wild rabbit, cut into 8–10 pieces (ask your butcher to do this)
2 tablespoons olive oil
1 bunch of thyme, leaves only
1 bunch of marjoram, chopped
pinch dried oregano
10 garlic cloves, thinly sliced
60ml (2fl oz) dry sherry

pinch saffron threads
100g (3½oz) blanched almonds, toasted
200g (7oz) diced red capsicum
2L (64fl oz) chicken stock
salt and pepper
400g (13oz) Calasparra rice

SHERRY AND JUNIPER MARINADE
60ml (2fl oz) olive oil
60ml (2fl oz) dry sherry
1 teaspoon dried juniper berries, lightly crushed
1 teaspoon black peppercorns
1 teaspoon salt flakes
1 head garlic, roughly chopped

To make sherry and juniper marinade, combine all ingredients in a large bowl.

Add rabbit pieces to the marinade. Toss to combine. Refrigerate, covered, overnight. Drain rabbit and pat dry with absorbent paper. Discard marinade.

Heat half the oil in a large, heavy based frying pan over high heat. Cook the rabbit in batches, for about 2 minutes on each side or until golden brown. Remove and set aside. Reduce heat.

Add remaining oil to same pan. Add thyme, marjoram, oregano and garlic. Cook, stirring, for 2 minutes—be careful not to burn the garlic.

Stir in sherry, saffron, almonds, peppers and stock. Season. Bring to a simmer. Add rabbit. Sprinkle rice evenly into pan.

Cook, over medium heat, without stirring, for about 25 minutes or until stock has been absorbed and rice is almost tender. Reduce heat to low and cook for a further 3 minutes to form a nice 'soccarrada'. If hob plate is not as big as pan, move pan around a little during cooking to ensure even heat.

You can also serve this dish with roasted garlic (see Basics & Sauces).

TIP: DO NOT USE FROZEN RABBIT OR THE MEAT WILL BE TOUGH—FRESH IS BEST.

A CREATIVE TAKE ON TRADITIONAL PAELLA, THIS DISH IS TYPICAL OF THE SOUTHERN CITY OF VALENCIA. THE CUTTLEFISH INK GIVES IT ITS DISTINCTIVE COLOUR AND THE AMAZING BOMBA RICE ABSORBS ALL THE MOUTHWATERING FLAVOURS WITHOUT BECOMING HEAVY OR GLUGGY. THE ONLY THING MISSING? A CHILLED GLASS OF CAVA TO WASH IT DOWN.

BLACK RICE WITH CUTTLEFISH AND GIANT PRAWNS 'MAESTRE STYLE'

Serves: 4
Prep time: 10 minutes
Cooking time: 20 minutes

400g (13oz) cleaned cuttlefish, scored
400g (13oz) king prawns, peeled, tails intact
1 tablespoon olive oil
2 garlic cloves, finely chopped
100g (3½oz) tomato puree
1 tablespoon sweet paprika
2L (64fl oz) fish or vegetable stock
1½ teaspoons calamari ink (available from your fishmonger)
pinch of saffron threads
400g (13oz) Bomba rice
salt and pepper

Cut cuttlefish and prawns into 2cm (½in) pieces.

Heat oil in a 25cm (10in) round paella pan. Add cuttlefish and prawns, and cook for 1 minute. Add garlic, puree and paprika. Cook, stirring, for about 1 minute or until fragrant. Stir in stock, ink and saffron. Bring to a boil.

Sprinkle rice evenly into pan. Season. Boil gently for 20 minutes, shaking pan occasionally. If hob plate is not as big as pan, move pan around a little during cooking to ensure even heat.

TIPS: BOMBA RICE IS A SHORT-GRAIN RICE FROM THE CALASPARRA REGION OF SPAIN. IT HAS THE ABILITY TO ABSORB COOKING LIQUID AND FORM A CRUST WHILE RETAINING ITS SHAPE. IF UNAVAILABLE, SUBSTITUTE WITH ANOTHER SHORT-GRAIN RICE. THE INK IS BETTER IF IT'S FRESH AND IN A TINY BAG INSIDE THE CUTTLEFISH.

Spanish passion is always reflected in our food. We cook from the heart.

The origins of this chunky vegetable hotpot lie in Spanish gypsy culture, taking advantage of seasonal produce. An economical dish that is filling and satisfying, the pears soak up the flavoursome juices becoming melt-in-your mouth tender. Serve it with thick sourdough toast and match with a glass of cider—the cloudier the better!

Olla Gitana con Peras

GYPSY VEGETABLE STEW WITH PEARS

Serves: 4
Prep time: 20 minutes + soaking time
Cook time: 1 hour 20 minutes

1L (32fl oz) vegetable stock

250g (8oz) dried chickpeas, soaked overnight

1 tablespoon olive oil

1 eschallot, thinly sliced

250g (8oz) butternut pumpkin, diced

250g (8oz) potatoes, diced chunky

1 very ripe tomato, quartered

1 teaspoon smoked paprika

pinch saffron threads

3 bay leaves

4 pears, cored, quartered

1 small eggplant, diced chunky

salt and pepper

250g (8oz) green beans, thinly sliced

chopped parsley, to garnish

Bring stock and chickpeas to boil in a large saucepan. Simmer, uncovered, for about 1 hour or until almost tender.

Meanwhile, heat oil in a small frying pan. Add eschallot, pumpkin and potatoes. Cook, stirring, until golden. Stir in tomato and paprika. Cook for 2 minutes. Stir in saffron and bay leaves.

Add potato mixture, pears and eggplant to chickpeas. Season. Bring to a boil.

Simmer uncovered, stirring occasionally, for about 30 minutes or until potatoes are tender.

Stir in green beans and remove from heat. Stand 15 minutes to allow beans to cook with residual heat from stew. Garnish with parsley.

TRADITIONAL SPANISH FISH BROTH

MY HOMETOWN OF MURCIA IS AN OLD FISHERMEN'S VILLAGE ON THE SOUTH COAST OF SPAIN. SEAFOOD IS FRESH AND AFFORDABLE AND AN ABSOLUTE FAVOURITE WITH THE LOCALS. THIS TRADITIONAL STEW, PACKED WITH FISH AND CRUSTACEANS, IS MADE RICH WITH THE ADDITION OF GROUND NUTS. IT SINGS OF WAVES LAPPING ON THE SAND—THE PERFECT SEASIDE LUNCH OR ROMANTIC DINNER. USE THE FRESHEST FISH YOU CAN FIND AND SERVE WITH A GLASS OF PINK MUSCAT TO COMPLETE THE CULINARY JOURNEY.

Serves: 4
Prep time: 25 minutes
Cooking time: 30 minutes

15 blanched almonds, toasted
1 tablespoon pine nuts, toasted
2 tablespoons olive oil
8 garlic cloves, thinly sliced
1 onion, finely chopped
1 bulb of fennel, finely chopped
1 tablespoon plain flour
500g (1lb) very ripe tomatoes,
* chopped*
½ bunch parsley, chopped

sprig of thyme
4 bay leaves
pinch spicy paprika
cracked pepper, to taste
250ml (8fl oz) white wine
2 tablespoons sherry
600ml (20fl oz) fish or vegetable stock
4 x 125g (4oz) white fish fillets
* (snapper, cod, barramundi)*

4 large king prawns, de-veined
1 blue swimmer crab, cleaned, quartered
1 cleaned calamari hood, cut into 3cm
* (1in)pieces*
10 black mussels, cleaned
salt and pepper

Preheat oven to 180°C (350°F).

Using a small grinder or mortar and pestle, crush almonds and pine nuts to a coarse paste.

Heat oil in a large flameproof baking dish. Add garlic, onion and fennel. Cook, stirring, for about 5 minutes or until fennel is soft. Stir in flour. Cook for 1 minute.

Stir in tomatoes, parsley, thyme, bay leaves, paprika, pepper, wine and sherry. Cook until liquid is reduced by half.

Add stock. Bring to a boil. Stir in nut paste and seafood. Season.

Cover dish tightly with foil. Cook in the oven for 20 minutes.

ROASTED POTATO HALVES

Serves: 2
Prep time: 5 minutes
Cooking time: 30 minutes

2 large potatoes
salt and pepper
80ml (2¾ fl oz) olive oil
3 sprigs of thyme, leaves only
ajo, to serve (see Basics &
    Sauces)

Preheat oven to 200°C (400°F).

Peel and cut potatoes in half. Score all over with a fork.

Place in a baking dish. Toss with salt, pepper, oil and thyme.

Cook for about approximately 30 minutes, turning half way through, or until golden brown, crisp and tender.

Serve potatoes with aioli or romesco marinade (see Basics & Sauces).

WHY BUY CHIPS WHEN THEY ARE SO EASY TO MAKE.

Potato Fries

POTATO FRIES

Serves: 2
Prep time: 5 minutes
Cooking time: 10 minutes

2 large potatoes
oil, for deep frying
sea salt

Thinly slice potatoes using a mandolin—you want them paper thin.

Deep fry in batches until golden and crisp.

Remove with a slotted spoon. Drain on absorbent paper. Season with salt.

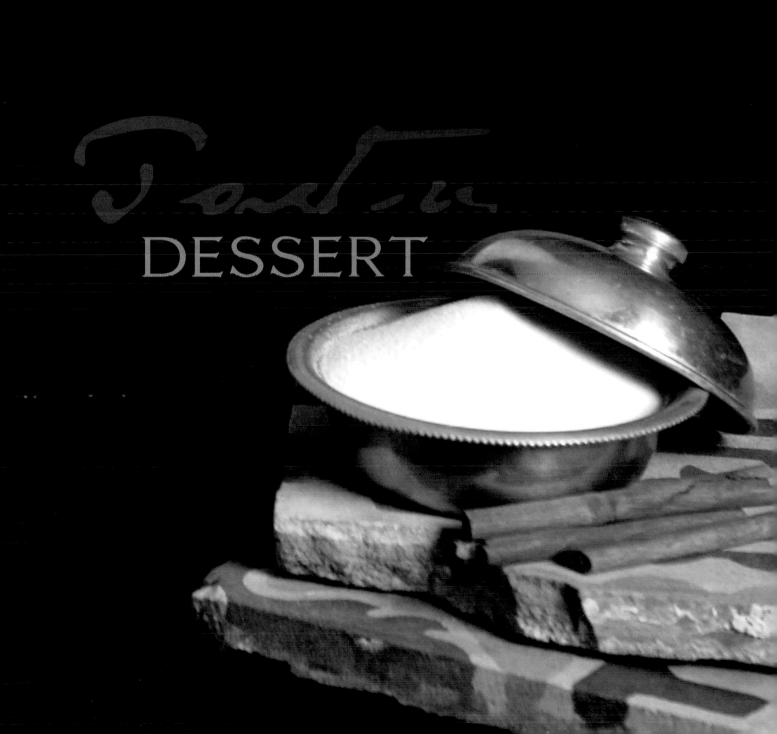

DESSERT

Translating as a 'slice of bacon from heaven', there is certainly no bacon in this creamy caramel delight. It is, however, definitely a slice of something ethereal!

Sunday's family dinner was at my auntie's house and she would make this velvety sweetness every week. I transformed into a perfectly behaved little boy (my mother knew better) from the moment I stepped through the door...the only way to secure second helpings.

We can't make this quickly enough in the restaurant and sell out every evening—I need a sideline business in chicken farming just to keep up with the egg supply

Tolino T Cielo

HEAVEN'S LITTLE PIG CARAMEL DELIGHT

Serves: 12–14
Prep time: 10 minutes
Cooking time: 1 hour 35 minutes + refrigeration

1kg (2lb) caster sugar
1L (32fl oz) water
2 vanilla beans, split, seeds
    scraped out
1 cinnamon quill
finely grated rind of 1 lemon
36 egg yolks

CARAMEL
250g (8oz) caster sugar
250ml (8fl oz) water

Preheat oven to 170°C (360°F).

To make caramel, stir sugar and water in a medium-sized, heavy based saucepan over medium heat, without boiling, until sugar dissolves. Use a wet pastry brush to brush any stray grains on side of pan back down into mixture. Bring to a boil. Boil, uncovered, without stirring, until mixture turns light golden brown. Pour into a deep 30cm (12in) round ovenproof dish or cake pan. Allow to set.

Stir sugar and water in a medium-sized heavy based saucepan over medium heat, without boiling, until sugar dissolves. Add vanilla beans and seeds, cinnamon and rind. Boil gently for about 15 minutes or until mixture thickens to a syrup and large bubbles appear on surface (you do not want syrup to colour). Strain through a sieve. Cool.

Whisk egg yolks in a large glass bowl until combined. Gradually beat in cooled syrup. Skim off any bubbles or froth, as you want the set custard to be smooth. Pour custard into dish over caramel.

Place round dish in a baking dish. Add enough boiling water to come half way up the outside of round dish. Cook in the oven for about 1 hour or until custard is just set. Cool 5 minutes. Remove round dish from baking dish. Cool to room temperature. Run a knife around edge of custard. Invert onto a plate.

Refrigerate overnight.

I love my milk—I drink over a litre a day! That's why I can't remember the last time I broke a bone. This recipe is a great way to build up your calcium. It is a very traditional recipe and very similar to crème pâtissière but with a lovely Spanish touch.

LIGHTLY FRIED MILK PÂTTISSIER

Serves: 4–6
Prep time: 30 minutes
Cooking time: 25 minutes + 2 hours refrigeration

1L (32fl oz) milk
60g (2oz) sugar
finely grated rind of 1 lemon
1 cinnamon stick
1 vanilla bean, split, seeds
   scraped out
100g (3½oz) plain flour
2 eggs
2 teaspoons butter
flour, for dusting
olive oil, for shallow frying

Grease a 25cm x 30cm (10in x 12in) Swiss roll pan. Line base with baking paper, extending paper 5cm (2in) over long sides of pan.

Bring milk, sugar, rind, cinnamon, vanilla beans and seeds to the boil in a medium saucepan. Remove from heat. Stand for at least 30 minutes to infuse. Strain and discard solids.

Place half the milk mixture in a medium-sized saucepan. Heat until warm.

Place flour in a small bowl. Slowly whisk in warm milk mixture. Whisk in eggs and butter.

Heat remaining milk mixture in saucepan. Add flour, milk and egg mixture. Stir with a spatula over a medium heat, for about 7 minutes or until smooth and thick.

Pour mixture into prepared pan. Smooth top with a wet spatula. Cool completely. Refrigerate for 2 hours.

Invert set custard onto a chopping board. Using a 7cm round cutter, cut out rounds.

Dust rounds with flour. Shallow fry until lightly golden. Drain on absorbent paper.

To serve, dust with castor sugar.

This is delicious served with crème anglaise (see Basics & Sauces).

My mother used to make small versions of this divine dessert and leave them in the fridge. Not a clever idea with three boys in the house! My brothers and I would sneak into the kitchen and hold surreptitious flan eating competitions. Judging was based on the all-important factors of speed and amount consumed! Carlos and Antonio were like custard-gobbling machines and I always came last...I think we need a rematch!

I have flavoured this beautiful custard with orange, but you can try using lemon, lime or even blood orange.

Flan

FRESH ORANGE SET CUSTARD

Serves: 6
Prep time: 25 minutes
Cooking time: 40 minutes

625ml (21fl oz) milk
2 vanilla beans, split, seeds
   scraped out
finely grated rind of
   2 oranges
3 eggs
2 egg yolks
160g (5¼oz) icing sugar

CARAMEL
220g (7oz) caster sugar
250ml (8 fl oz) water
1 tablespoon cointreau
½ tablespoon orange juice

Preheat oven to 170°C (360°F). Place six 13cm x 3cm (5in x 5in) deep round ovenproof dishes on an oven tray.

To make caramel, stir sugar and water in a medium-sized heavy based saucepan over medium heat, without boiling, until sugar dissolves. Use a wet pastry brush to brush any stray grains on side of pan back down into mixture. Bring to a boil. Boil, uncovered, without stirring, until mixture begins to turn light golden brown. Add cointreau and juice. Stir until dissolved.

Pour ½cm caramel into each ovenproof dish. Allow to set.

To make the custard, stir milk, vanilla beans and seeds and rind in a medium saucepan over low heat until boiling. Remove from heat. Stand 5 minutes. Remove vanilla beans.

Lightly whisk eggs, egg yolks and sifted icing sugar in a medium-sized bowl until combined.

Gradually whisk milk mixture into egg mixture. Divide evenly among dishes.

Cook in the oven for about 30 minutes in a bain marie. Cool to room temperature. Refrigerate overnight.

Run a knife around edge of custards. Invert onto serving plates.

Tip: A bain-marie is a cooking technique that enables the gentle transmission of heat to the dish for slow cooking through water.

This little gem is perfect for using up your once-delicious sourdough that has gone hard and stale. Revive and transform it into a silky bread and butter pudding laced with the scent of fresh vanilla and thyme. Invented by paupers but fit for a king!

BREAD AND BUTTER PUDDING

Serves: 4
Prep time: 20 minutes
Cooking time: 40 minutes

500ml (17fl oz) milk
1 tablespoon Pedro Ximenez
    sherry
4 eggs
250g (8oz) caster sugar
½ bunch thyme, leaves only
2 vanilla beans, split, seeds
    scraped out
8–10 slices sourdough bread,
    without the crust
extra caster sugar, to sprinkle

Lightly grease four ovenproof dishes (200ml/6½fl oz capacity).

Whisk milk, Pedro Ximenez, eggs, sugar, thyme and vanilla seeds in a large jug until combined.

Cut bread to size to fit prepared dishes. Cover sides and bottom of dish. Pour over milk mixture. Stand for about 2 hours or until bread is very soft. Then wrap the dishes in plastic wrap and make sure its very airtight.

Place dishes in a baking dish. Add enough boiling water to come half way up the outside of ovenproof dishes.

Cook in the oven for about 45 minutes at 145°C (265°F) or until puddings are just set.

Run a thin-bladed knife around outside of puddings and turn out onto an oven tray. Sprinkle puddings with extra sugar. Cook under a hot grill or use a domestic blow torch to caramelise sugar until golden brown.

Tip: I used 11cm x 3cm (4in x 1in) round dishes. The exact amount of bread will depend on the size of your loaf.

A CHILDHOOD FAVOURITE, THE CINNAMON, CITRUS AND VANILLA AROMAS OF THIS PUDDING TRANSPORT ME STRAIGHT BACK TO THE KITCHEN TABLE WHEN I WAS A SMALL BOY. RICH, CREAMY AND SATISFYING, THIS IS ESPECIALLY POPULAR IN THE NORTH OF SPAIN WHERE DAIRY FARMS ARE ABUNDANT. A PERFECT ALL ROUNDER—EAT IT WARM ON A WINTER'S EVE OR CHILLED ON A SUMMER'S DAY. EVEN BETTER, IT HAPPILY SITS IN THE REFRIGERATOR FOR AT LEAST THREE DAYS. FOR A SPECIAL OCCASION, SPRINKLE IT WITH SUGAR AND COOK UNDER A HOT GRILL FOR A CARAMEL BRULEE TOP.

CREAMY CINAMON AND CITRUS RICE PUDDING

Serves: 4–6
Prep time: 5 minutes
Cook time: 35 minutes

rind of 2 oranges
rind of 2 lemons
1L (32fl oz) full-fat milk
200g (7oz) Calasparra rice
165g (5½ oz) caster sugar
2 vanilla beans, split, seeds
   scraped out
1 cinnamon quill
pinch of salt
125ml (4fl oz) full-fat cream
finely grated rind of
   1 blood orange
2 tablespoons caster sugar,
   extra

Rinse a medium-sized heavy based saucepan with cold water but don't dry it.

Add milk and rice to pan. Bring to a boil over medium heat.

Reduce heat. Stir in rind, sugar, vanilla beans and seeds, cinnamon quill and salt. Simmer, stirring occasionally, for about 30 minutes or until pudding is thick and creamy and rice is tender. Remove from heat. Stir in cream. Remove vanilla beans and cinnamon. Divide mixture among four flameproof ramekins, 13cm round x 3cm deep (5in x 1in).

Combine blood orange rind and extra sugar in a small bowl. Sprinkle over puddings. Cook under a hot grill until sugar melts and caramelises (you can use a kitchen blow torch if you have one).

Serve rice puddings with mandarin segments.

TIP: SERVE WITH MANDARIN SEGMENTS DRIZZLED WITH LAVENDER HONEY, AVAILABLE FROM GOOD DELICATESSENS.

Almond tarts are not just served for dessert in Spain. Chances are you'll find one at any Spanish takeaway coffee bar where it will be enjoyed with the list of endless coffees that the Spaniards have every day. Santiago de Compostela is the name of the patron of the trip across Spain that pilgrims do every year. He has a characteristic cross that decorates the top of the tart when the sugar is dusted on the tart to finish.

SANTIAGO'S TART

Serves: 6–8
Prep time: 20 minutes
Cooking time: 45 minutes

250g (8oz) plain flour
75g (2½oz) icing sugar
125g (4oz) cold butter,
  chopped
3 egg yolks
pinch salt

FILLING

125g (4oz) unsalted butter
50g (1¾oz) caster sugar
2 eggs
100g (3½oz) almond meal
1 teaspoon plain flour
finely grated rind of 1 orange
finely grated rind of 1 lemon
75g (2½oz) chocolate chips
icing sugar, to dust
double cream, to serve

Preheat oven to 175°C (360°F). Grease a 24cm (10in) round, loose-based, flan tin.

Sift flour and icing sugar into a processor. Add butter. Process until crumbly. Add yolks and salt. Process until ingredients just come together. Wrap dough in plastic wrap. Refrigerate for 1 hour.

Roll dough between two sheets of baking paper until large enough to line prepared tin. Lift dough into tin and press it into sides. Refrigerate for 15 minutes. Line with baking paper. Fill with rice or baking beans. Cook in the oven for 10 minutes. Remove paper and rice. Return to oven for about a further 3 minutes or until tart shell is dry and lightly browned. Cool.

To make filling, beat butter and sugar in small bowl of electric mixer until light and creamy. Add eggs one at a time, beating between additions. Stir in almond meal, flour, rind and chocolate chips. Spoon filling into tart shell.

Cook in the oven for about 30–35 minutes or until the tip of a knife comes out clean when inserted. Cool completely.

Dust with sifted icing sugar. Serve with cream.

Tip: If you struggle to put the pastry into the flan tin, roll it between two sheets of plastic wrap instead of baking paper, pull off the top sheet, invert the pie dough into the pan and peel off the second sheet. Alternatively, roll out the dough into small pieces and patch them together in the tin with floured fingers.

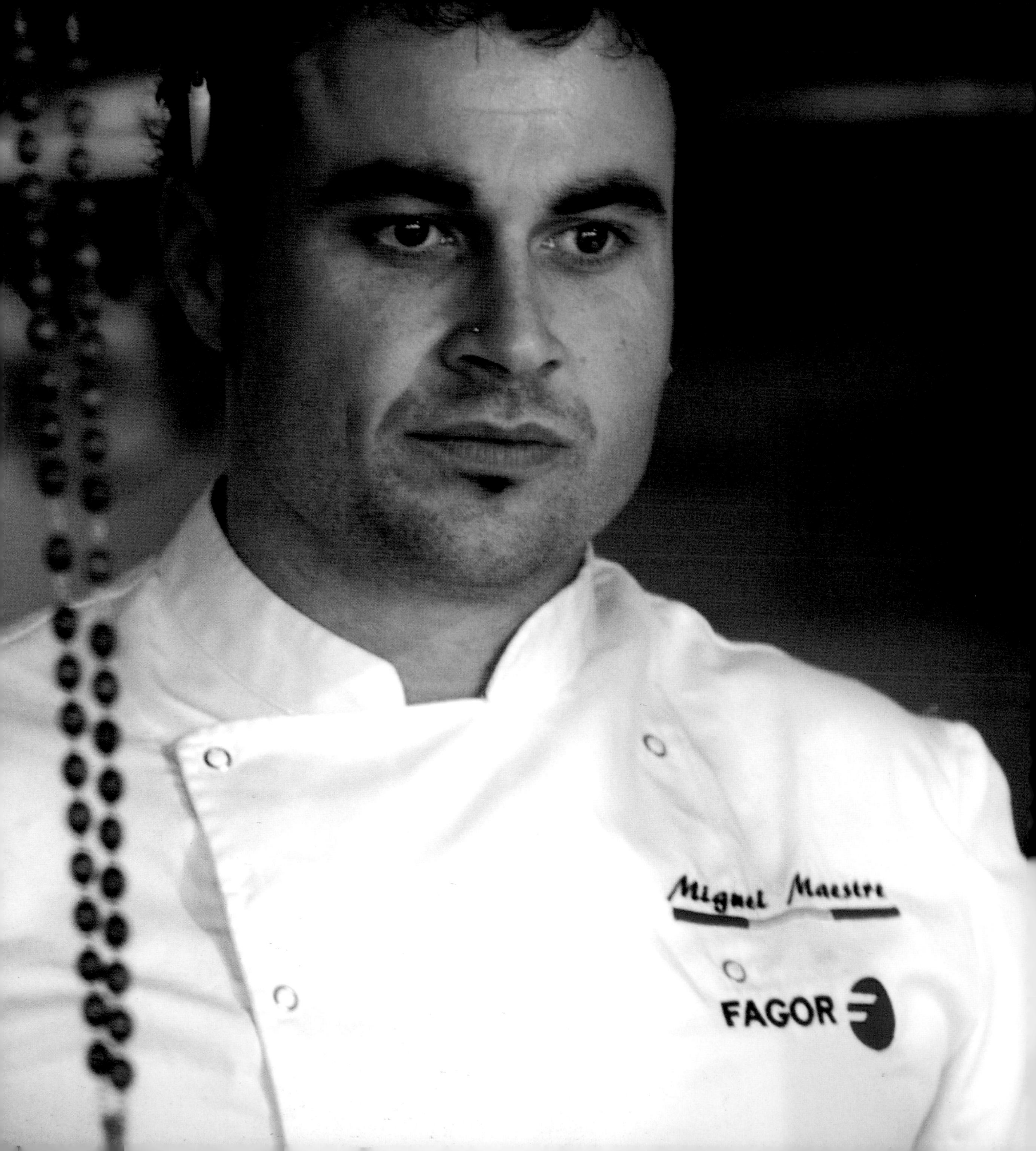
Miguel Maestre
FAGOR

AFTERNOON TEA

PERFECT WITH TOASTED BREAD AND GHERKINS, WE COOK THIS FRESH EVERY DAY IN THE RESTAURANT. THIS IS A VERY DELICATE RECIPE SO MAKE SURE YOU FOLLOW THE COOKING TIME CLOSELY.

Jate de Higado de Pato

DUCK LIVER PATE

Serves: 4-6
Prep time: 20 minutes
Cooking time: 30 minutes + 3 hours refrigeration

200g (7oz) fresh duck livers
1 garlic clove
1 sprig thyme
1 pink eschallot
20ml (1fl oz) Pedro Ximenez
   sherry
1 teaspoon salt
pinch pepper
1 pinch nitrate (available from
   your butcher)
200g (7oz) butter, at room
   temperature
2 eggs, at room temperature
cracked pepper and extra fresh
   thyme, to garnish

JELLY
1 gelatine leaf
1 tablespoon honey
1 tablespoon sherry vinegar
25ml (1fl oz) water

Preheat oven to 120°C (250°F).

Trim any sinew from the livers. Rinse under cold water. Drain. Pat dry with absorbent paper.

Place livers, garlic, thyme, eschallot, sherry, salt, pepper and nitrate in a processor. Process until smooth. Add butter in four batches, processing between additions. Add eggs one at a time, processing between additions.

Pass mixture through a sieve into a jug.

Divide mixture among four ovenproof dishes (12cm/4.5in diameter), leaving 0.5cm (¼in) at the top for the jelly. Place dishes in a baking dish. Add enough boiling water to come half way up the outside of dishes.

Cook in the oven for 30 minutes. Cool 5 minutes. Remove dishes from baking dish. Cool to room temperature. Refrigerate.

To make jelly, soak gelatine leaf in water until soft. Remove and squeeze out water. Place the gelatine in a small saucepan with honey, vinegar and water. Stir over a low heat until gelatine is dissolved and mixture is hot. Cool to room temperature. Pour over pate in dishes. Garnish with pepper and thyme. Refrigerate for 3 hours or overnight.

Serve pate with toasted bread.

TIPS: MAKE SURE LIVERS ARE VERY FRESH AND ALL INGREDIENTS ARE ROOM TEMPERATURE WHEN MAKING THIS RECIPE. TO KEEP THE PATE PINK INSIDE, USE NITRATE—YOU CAN FIND IT IN ANY BUTCHER SHOP.

My trick for tender octopus is freezing it for 2 weeks, allowing the muscle to begin to break down and become tender. If you don't have 2 weeks, you can buy octopus already tenderised from your fishmonger or, even better, follow my boyhood instructions. Go spear fishing with your uncle to find your eight-legged catch—no mean feat. With tentacled prize in hand, smack it against the rocks for about 10 minutes to soften the meat. Beware, however, of retaliation—my last catch bit a nice little chunk out of my arm. It was worth it and made the tastiest Pulpo a la Gallega I have ever made.

Pulpo a la Gallega

GALICIAN-STYLE OCTOPUS

Serves: 4
Prep time: 10 minutes
Cooking time: 2–3 hours

3 bay leaves fresh
1kg (2lb) octopus (frozen for
    15 days), thawed
salt and pepper
25ml (1fl oz) chilli oil
1 teaspoon hot paprika
150ml (5fl oz) olive oil
10 flat leaf parsley leaves
1 lemon, cut into wedges

Bring a large saucepan of water to a boil with bay leaves. Add octopus. Simmer, topping up water as necessary, for 2–3 hours or until very tender. Drain. Cool.

Using a small sharp knife, slice octopus into chunky pieces. Arrange on a plate and season. Drizzle with oil and sprinkle with paprika.

Pat parsley leaves dry with absorbent paper (any moisture will make oil spit). Heat oil in a small saucepan. Fry parsley leaves in batches until crisp. Drain on absorbent paper.

Serve octopus with a squeeze of fresh lemon. Garnish with deep-fried parsley leaves.

Dinner in Spain is a late affair, but before this, around 6pm, is a time called Merienda, a sort of late afternoon tea time. This is the perfect hour to sneak in an empanadilla and an icy cold beer. The pastry is made with olive oil and white wine, and crumbles in the mouth like a savoury shortbread. This large version is perfect for family dinners.

EMPANADILLAS

Serves: 6
Prep time: 15 minutes
Cooking time: 50 minutes

1 tablespoon olive oil

1 large onion, thinly sliced

375g (13oz) plain flour

375g (13oz) strong bread flour

2 teaspoons salt

1 teaspoon paprika

250ml (8fl oz) extra virgin olive oil

250ml (8fl oz) white wine

300g passata

3 hard boiled eggs, chopped

100g (3½oz) fresh or frozen peas

425g (13½ oz) can tuna in olive oil, drained

2 piquillo peppers, sliced julienne

4 cornichons or capers, sliced

1 egg, lightly beaten

Preheat oven to 180°C (350°F). Line an oven tray with baking paper.

Heat oil in a small frying pan. Cook onion until soft and golden brown. Set aside.

Sift flours, salt and paprika into a large bowl. Stir in combined oil and wine to form a soft dough (you can do this in a mixer with a dough attachment if you have one).

Divide dough in half. Stretch half over base and sides of a 24cm (10in) round, loose-based, flan tin. Line with baking paper. Fill with rice or baking beans. Cook in the oven for 10 minutes. Remove paper and rice. Cool.

Spread with passata. Top with cooked onions, eggs, peas, tuna, peppers and cornichons.

Stretch the other half of the dough into a 24cm (10in) circle and top the pie. Trim edges and press with a fork to seal. Make three holes on top of the pastry to let steam out.

Brush empanadillas with egg. Cook in the oven for about 40 minutes or until pastry is golden and cooked.

Serve hot or cold.

Tips: Traditionally I would use confit (tuna loin cooked very slowly in olive oil), but it is sometimes hard to find. Use the best quality canned tuna in oil available. You can make this as a free-form pie or as individual pies if you prefer.

The Murcians, like the Aussies, make spectacular meat pies, and no visit to the city is complete without one. Golden puff pastry encasing a delicious filling—they must be eaten freshly baked. My version uses wagyu beef which is marbled with fat, resulting in an intense flavour and succulent filling. No tomato sauce required!

WAGYU AND CHORIZO MEAT PIE

Serves: 4
Prep time: 30 minutes
Cooking time: 2 hours + 1.5 hours cooking

400g (13oz) wagyu scotch beef or skirt steak, cut into 3cm (1in) cubes
2 teaspoons plain flour
2 tablespoons extra virgin olive oil
1 carrot, diced
1 onion, diced
1 leek, thinly sliced
4 garlic cloves chopped
5 black peppercorns, crushed
200g (7oz) chorizo, diced
1 bunch thyme, leaves only
800ml (27fl oz) red wine
500ml (17fl oz) beef stock
4 sheets frozen puff pastry, thawed
1 egg, lightly beaten
4 hard boiled eggs, quartered

Toss beef and flour in a medium bowl.

Heat half the oil in a medium-sized saucepan until very hot. Add beef in batches. Cook until browned all over. Set aside.

Reduce heat. Add remaining oil to same pan. Add carrot, onion, leek, garlic, peppercorns, chorizo and thyme. Cook, stirring occasionally, for about 10 minutes or until vegetables are soft.

Return beef to pan with wine. Cook until liquid is reduced by half. Add stock. Bring to boil. Simmer for about 1.5 hours or until meat is tender and mixture is thick and no stock is left. Cool completely.

Preheat oven to 200°C (400°F). Grease four pie tins (8cm/3½in base measurement).

Cut 8 x 13cm (4½ in) circles from pastry. Line bases and sides of pans with half the circles. Trim edges. Line with baking paper. Fill with rice or baking beans. Cook in the oven for 10 minutes. Remove paper and rice. Brush with egg. Bake for 8 minutes. Cool.

Divide filling and eggs among pastry cases. Top with the remaining pastry rounds. Trim the edges and press with a fork to seal. Brush with egg. Cook for about 15 minutes or until pastry is puffed and golden brown, and filling is hot.

Tips: Beef filling can be made up to two days ahead. Store, covered, in the refrigerator.

Use fresh puff pastry if you can find it. It is so much better.

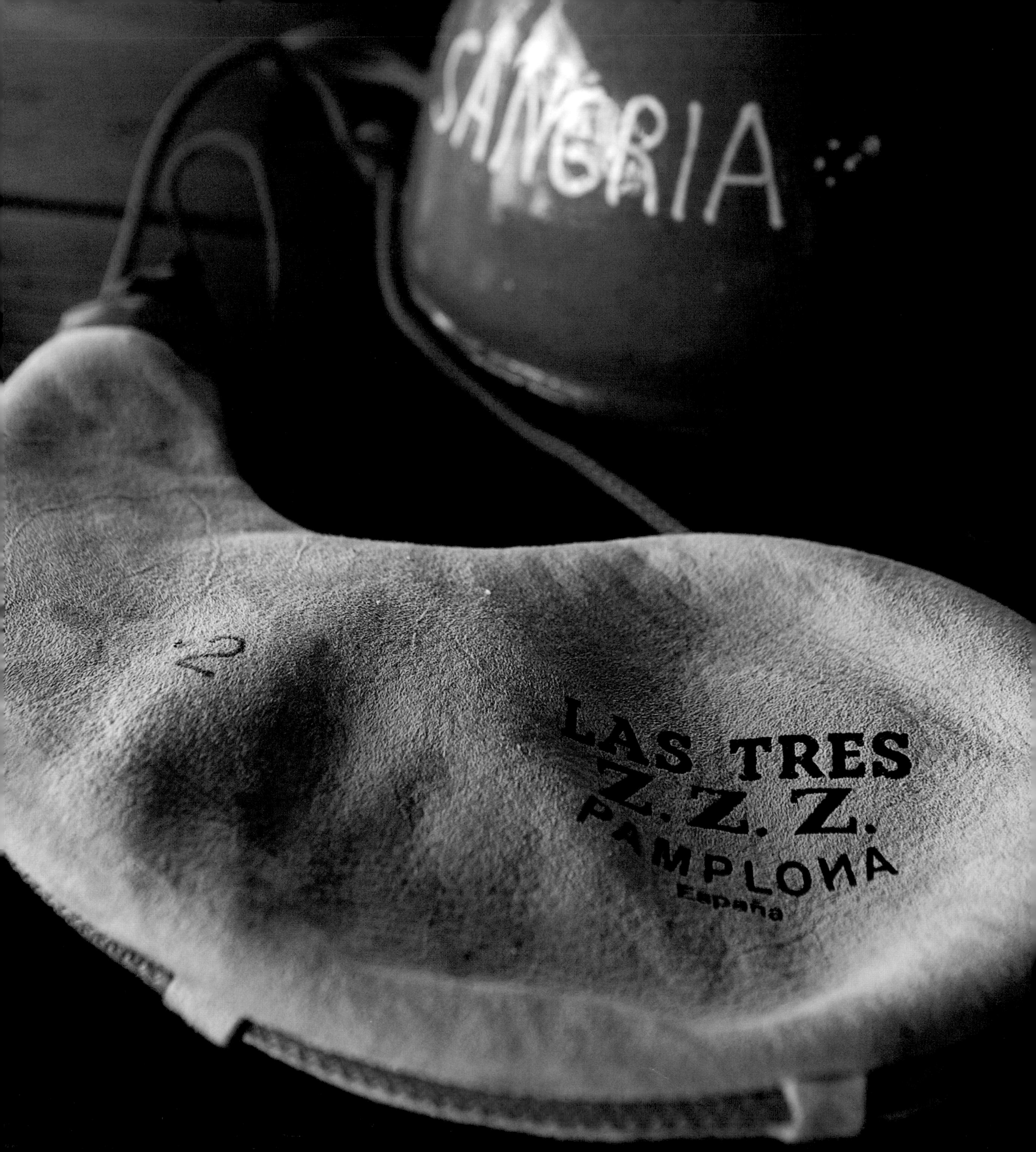
SANGRIA
2
LAS TRES
Z.Z.Z.
PAMPLONA
España

Pastel actually translates as 'cake', though this creation is really more of a pie. Around 70 years ago a Russian ship ran into trouble off Mar Menor (a salty lagoon in south-east Murcia). While the ship was being repaired the ship's cook struck up a friendship with the local patissier and shared his recipe for a savoury pie made with sweet pastry.

My grandfather was entertaining the Murcian politician Juan de la Cierva at the time, and the patissier presented the pie at one of their esteemed dinners. So impressed was the politician that he asked for it to be made whenever he visited. The patissier honoured the complement by naming the pie after him.

It is now eaten throughout Murcia and I have made it in the very kitchen in which it was invented. It makes me proud to be a Maestre.

SWEET AND SAVOURY CHICKEN PIE

Serves: 4–6
Prep time: 40 minutes
Cooking time: 1hour 40 minutes

1 chicken
250g (8oz) pork fat or lard, at room temperature
250g (8oz) caster sugar
finely grated rind of 1 lemon
2 eggs
450g (13½oz) plain flour
2 boiled eggs, chopped
1 egg extra, lightly beaten

Preheat oven to 200°C (400°F).

Place chicken in a large saucepan or stockpot. Cover with cold salted water. Bring to a boil. Simmer gently for about 1 hour or until cooked through. Remove from heat. Stand 30 minutes. Remove chicken, reserving 1 cup of the liquid. Refrigerate until cold. Remove and shred meat. Combine meat with enough of the reserved liquid to give a slightly wet consistency.

Place pork fat and sugar in large bowl of an electric mixer. Using the paddle attachment beat until light and fluffy. Beat in rind. Add eggs one at a time, beating between additions. Add flour gradually. Beat to just combine and form a dry-ish dough.

Roll half the dough between two sheets of baking paper until large enough to line base and side of a 24cm (10in) round, loose-based, flan tin. Blind bake for 10 minutes. Fill with chicken and boiled eggs.

Roll remaining dough between two sheets of baking paper until large enough to cover pie. Trim edges and press with a fork to seal. Brush with egg.

Cook in the oven for about 40 minutes or until pastry is golden and crisp.

Eat the same day as cooked.

DINNER

To call yourself a Spaniard, you must be able to make your own chorizo—or at least attempt to make it—the most iconical sausage in the history of Spain. My grandfather taught me the easiest way to make them at home and to enjoy them with a cold beer We used to make the matanza with pigs over 200 kilograms into batches of more than 50 kilograms of chorizo. In my restaurant 50kg of chorizo will go in one Friday night dinner service.

Chorizo Casero

HOMEMADE CHORIZO

Serves: 2
Prep time: 20 minutes + overnight refrigeration
Cooking time: 40 minutes

200g (7oz) pork fillet, coarsely minced
25g (1½ tablespoons) pork fat, finely minced
1 teaspoon hot paprika
2 teaspoons sweet paprika
1 teaspoon smoked paprika
2 garlic cloves, finely chopped
pinch white pepper
pinch ground fennel
splash extra virgin olive oil
skin from one duck neck (ask your butcher for this)

Combine all ingredients except duck neck in a large bowl. Refrigerate, covered, overnight.

Tie duck neck skin at one end with butcher's twine.

Spoon pork mixture into a piping bag. Pipe all mixture into the duck neck. Tie end with twine. Trim. Wrap sausage in plastic wrap and then foil.

Cook in a steamer for 40 minutes. Cool. Remove plastic wrap and foil.

Cook in a hot frying pan until skin is crisp. Slice thickly and cook in a hot oven for 2 minutes before serving.

Tip: If you do not have an electric steamer, place a bamboo steamer over a wok or saucepan of simmering water. Place sausage parcel in steamer. Steam, covered, for 30-40 minutes or until firm, topping up water in wok or saucepan as necessary.

To call yourself a
Spaniard you must be
able to make your own chorizo.

This pasta dish has its origins in Valencia and is bursting with flavour and colour. It is cooked paella-style but uses pasta instead of rice. A great dish for sharing!

SEAFOOD FIDEUA

Serves: 4
Prep time: 10 minutes
Cooking time: 45 minutes

1 tablespoon extra virgin olive oil

1 red capsicum, roughly chopped

1 yellow capsicum, roughly chopped

1 red onion, finely chopped

1 garlic clove, chopped

2 teaspoons smoked paprika

2 teaspoons spicy paprika

2 mud crabs, cleaned and quartered

3 calamari, cut into rings

375g (13oz) gomiti or fussilli pasta

pinch of saffron threads

3 tomatoes, chopped

500ml (17fl oz) white wine

500ml (17fl oz) fish stock

½ bunch parsley, finely chopped

Heat oil in a large, deep paella pan. Cook capsicums, onion and garlic, stirring, until onion is soft.

Stir in paprikas. Stir in crabs and calamari. Add pasta, saffron and tomatoes. Stir to combine. Add wine. Cook for 2 minutes to reduce slightly. Stir in stock and parsley. Bring to a boil. Simmer, uncovered, for about 30 minutes or until no stock left.

Tips: Gomiti is a short c-shaped pasta tube, sometimes called elbow macaroni. You can use any type of short pasta, such as orecchiette, farfalle, fusilli or regular macaroni.

Smash the cloves of crab with the back of a knife to get the sauce through the crab meat.

I LOVE THE IDEA OF WRAPPING UP A MYRIAD OF FLAVOURS AND TEXTURES IN ONE CLEVER PARCEL. THESE ARE ALSO A HEALTHY CHOICE THAT WILL HELP YOU WATCH YOUR WAISTLINE WITHOUT COMPROMISING ON TASTE. I RECENTLY MADE A BATCH FOR A PARTY, BUT AFTER 'TESTING' ONE, FOUND I HAD SCOFFED THE LOT BEFORE ANYONE EVEN ARRIVED. WHAT CAN I SAY…'THE PROOF IS IN THE PUDDING'…OR CABBAGE ROLLS IN THIS CASE.

CHICKEN CABBAGE PARCELS

Serves: 2
Prep time: 10 minutes
Cooking time: 7 minutes

6 Chinese cabbage leaves
200g (7oz) chicken mince
2 garlic cloves, finely chopped
1 pink eschallot, finely
    chopped
1 long fresh red chilli, finely
    chopped
1cm (½in) piece fresh ginger,
    finely chopped
¼ bunch coriander, finely
    chopped
2 teaspoons balsamic vinegar
40g (1¼oz) crushed almonds
coriander leaves, to garnish
olive oil and balsamic vinegar,
    to serve

Blanch cabbage leaves in boiling water in two batches, for about 1 minute or until softened. Remove with tongs. Refresh in iced water. Drain on absorbent paper.

Combine chicken, garlic, eschallot, chilli, ginger, coriander and vinegar in a bowl.

Divide mixture among centre of each cabbage leave. Sprinkle with nuts. Fold in sides of leaves and roll up tightly to enclose filling.

Place a bamboo steamer over a wok or saucepan of simmering water. Place cabbage parcels, seam-side down, in steamer. Steam, covered, for about 5 minutes or until chicken is cooked through.

Garnish cabbage parcels with coriander. Serve drizzled with olive oil and vinegar or black olive vinaigrette (see Basics & Sauces).

Good food, like good things, takes time.

VEAL SWEETBREADS

This tapas is a fiesta of contrasting flavours and textures—rich sweetbreads, sweet onions, crisp potato and creamy eggs. Veal sweetbreads are not always easy to find, but this dish makes it worth ordering them in advance from your butcher (lamb can be used as a substitute).

Serves: 4–6
Prep time: 10 minutes + 30 minutes soaking
Cooking time: 30 minutes

SWEETBREADS

1kg (4½lb) veal or lamb sweetbreads,
  trimmed, rinsed
1 onion, peeled
1 stalk celery
1 carrot, peeled
10 white peppercorns, crushed
10 black peppercorns, crushed
4 sprigs of thyme
½ bunch parsley
200ml (6½fl oz) white wine
salt and pepper
1L (32fl oz) chicken stock
2 tablespoons olive oil
parsley and lemon rind, to garnish

CARAMELISED ONIONS

50g (2oz) butter
4 onions, thinly sliced
1 tablespoon brown sugar
2 garlic cloves chopped
250ml (8fl oz) sherry
350ml (11.5fl oz) red wine

CRISPY PATATAS FRITAS

2 large desiree potatoes, thinly sliced
vegetable oil, for deep frying
pinch of sweet paprika
salt

POACHED EGGS

1L (32fl oz) water
1 teaspoon salt
splash white vinegar
splash of lemon juice
2 large very fresh free-range eggs

To make caramelised onions, melt butter in a large frying pan over medium heat. Add onions and cook, stirring occasionally, until very soft. Add sugar and garlic. Cook until golden brown. Increase heat. Add sherry in four batches, cooking until evaporated between additions. Repeat with red wine. Onions should be soft, rich and thick at the end of cooking. Remove from heat. Cover to keep warm.

To prepare sweetbreads, soak them in cold salted water for 30 minutes. Drain.

Place onion, celery and carrot in a processor. Process until finely chopped.

Place vegetable mixture, peppercorns, thyme, parsley, wine, salt and pepper and stock in a large saucepan. Bring to a boil. Simmer for 15 minutes. Season.

Add sweetbreads. Simmer gently for 10 minutes. Remove from heat. Cool completely. Remove sweetbreads with a slotted spoon and discard liquid.

Remove and discard sweetbread membranes and skin. Drain sweetbreads on absorbent paper. Cut into 2cm (½in slices).

To make crispy patatas fritas, deep fry potato slices in batches until crisp and golden. Drain on absorbent paper. Season with salt and paprika.

To poach eggs, bring water, salt, vinegar and juice to boil in a medium saucepan. Crack the eggs into two glasses so it is easier to pour them into the water. Stir the water clockwise and with the water still turning, add the eggs. Cook for 2 minutes. Remove with a slotted spoon. Drain on absorbent paper.

To finish the sweetbreads, heat olive oil in a heavy-based frying pan. Cook them until crisp. Served with patatas fritas, caramelised onions and poached eggs. Garnish with parsley and lemon rind.

I USE GOW GEE WRAPPERS TO MAKE THESE DELICATE CABALLITOS BECAUSE THEY ARE QUICK AND EASY AND THERE JUST ISN'T ALWAYS TIME TO MAKE YOUR OWN PASTA. THE CHUNKY PESTO IS A TOTAL WINNER AND PAIRS PERFECTLY WITH THE SWEETNESS OF THE PRAWNS.

THIS IS MY ONLY NON-TRADITIONAL TAPA IN THE BOOK, BUT I LOVE GOW-GEE AND I REALLY WANTED TO SHARE THIS RECIPE. OPEN YOUR MIND.

Caballitos en Gow-Gee

PRAWN GOW-GEE SPANISH STYLE

Serves: 1
Prep time: 5 minutes
Cooking time: 10 minutes

8 gow-gee pastry wrappers
4 king prawns, shelled, de-veined
1 tablespoon olive oil
1 small bunch spinach, washed, chopped
lime wedges, to serve

PESTO

2 bunches coriander
2 bunches basil
100g (3½oz) pine nuts
1 garlic clove
0.5cm piece fresh ginger
4 teaspoons olive oil
½ long fresh red chilli

To make pesto, place all ingredients in a small processor. Pulse until mixture is combined but still chunky.

To make caballitos, place four gow gee wrappers on a work surface.

Bend each prawn into a circle, and place in centre of wrapper.

Top each prawn with a teaspoon of pesto. Brush edges of wrappers with water. Top with remaining wrappers, pressing edges to seal.

Cook caballitos in a saucepan of boiling, salted water for 2–3 minutes or until wrappers are translucent. Remove with a slotted spoon.

Heat olive oil in a large frying pan. Cook spinach for about 1 minute or until wilted.

Arrange spinach on serving plate. Top with caballitos. Serve with lime wedges and remaining pesto.

TIP: FREEZE ANY LEFTOVER PESTO IN ICE-CUBE TRAYS TO USE LATER.

Traditionally served to farm workers for lunch, this hearty stew is designed to replenish and refuel. It is a signature dish in my restaurant, El Toro Loco, and harks back to my childhood when my mother made it every week. In Spain it is served as two dishes, with the stock as entree, and the meat and chickpeas as the main course. Fresh sourdough bread fried in olive oil makes an excellent tool to mop up the juices. Two of its best attributes? It gets better after a couple of days in the refrigerator and is the best hangover cure.

Sydney Weekender awarded this recipe the best chickpea dish of the year.

CHICKPEA AND PORK HOTPOT

Serves: 4–6
Prep time: 15 minutes
Cooking time: 30 minutes

4 chorizo sausages, thickly sliced

100g (3½oz) piece jamon Serrano, diced

100g (3½oz) piece salami, diced

100g (3½oz) piece pancetta, diced

5 garlic cloves, sliced

5 pink eschallots, quartered

1 bunch of thyme, leaves only

2 x 400g (13oz) tins chickpeas, drained

100g (3½oz) of morcilla, sliced (optional)

2L (64oz) beef stock

1 bunch parsley, chopped

Heat a large saucepan. Add chorizo, jamon, salami and pancetta. Cook, stirring occasionally, over a medium heat for about 10 minutes or until lightly browned and the fat in the meat has started to break down.

Add garlic, eschallots and thyme. Cook, stirring occasionally, for about 10 minutes or until eschallots are very soft.

Stir in chickpeas and morcilla. Cook, stirring occasionally, for 5 minutes so chickpeas can absorb flavours from meat and thyme. Stir in stock. Bring to a boil. Simmer, for about 1 hour or until slightly thickened.

Garnish stew with parsley.

A WINTER WARMER THAT RANKS AS ONE OF MY ALL-TIME FAVOURITES. IT CAN BE MADE UP TO THREE DAYS IN ADVANCE AND THE LONG, SLOW BRAISING MAKES THE MEAT MELTINGLY TENDER—TRUE SPANISH COMFORT FOOD. I MAKE IT IN BIG BATCHES THEN FREEZE IN INDIVIDUAL PORTIONS—GREAT FOR A NO-FUSS DINNER PARTY. SERVE WITH CREAMY MASH AND A FEISTY RIOJA TO KEEP THOSE WINTER CHILLS AT BAY.

Codillo de Cordero al Vino Tinto

LAMB SHANKS A LA ESPAÑOLA

Serves: 2
Prep time: 20 minutes
Cooking time: 2 hours + marinating

2 large lamb shanks
1L (32fl oz) red wine
2 tablespoons olive oil
1 stick celery, coarsely chopped
1 onion, coarsely chopped
1 leek, coarsely chopped
1 fresh, long red chilli, finely chopped
1 head of garlic, cloves separated and peeled
2 tablespoons coarsely chopped sage
2 tablespoons thyme leaves
1 pig's trotter
500ml (17fl oz) beef stock
salt and pepper

Combine lamb and half the wine in a medium bowl. Refrigerate, covered, overnight. Drain lamb and discard wine.

Preheat oven to 180°C (350°F).

Heat half the oil in a medium-sized flameproof casserole dish until very hot. Add lamb. Cook, turning, until browned all over. Remove and set aside. Reduce heat.

Add remaining oil to same dish. Add mirepoix (celery, onion, leek), chilli, garlic, sage and thyme. Cook, stirring, until vegetables are very soft.

Add remaining wine. Bring to a boil, stirring to remove any crusty bits from base of dish. Simmer until reduced by half. Return lamb to dish with pig's trotter (the trotter's natural gelatine will thicken the sauce to give a rich braising liquid) and stock. Season. Bring to a boil.

Transfer to oven. Cook, covered, for 1–3 hours or until sauce is thick and lamb falls off bone.

TIP: FOR THE PERFECT ACCOMPANIMENT, FRY THINLY SLICED KIPFLER POTATOES IN OLIVE OIL WITH A VERY HOT CHILLI UNTIL GOLDEN AND CRISP.

This is road trip food Mamá Maestre style! With a family full of boys and large appetites, my mother would make a vat of this for the journey to our holiday house every summer. A roadside stop-off would see us devour a couple of kilos of these addictive lamb chops in a few minutes.

Chuletas de Cordero al Ajo Cabañil

LAMB CHOPS WITH GARLIC

Serves: 4
Prep time: 10 minutes
Cooking time: 10 minutes

80ml (2¾fl oz) olive oil
500g (1lb) kipfler potaotes, cut into 1cm (¼in) thick slices
salt and pepper
8 lamb loin chops
100ml (3½fl oz) beef stock
2 tablespoons white wine vinegar
1 tablespoon caster sugar
10 garlic cloves, chopped
mint leaves, to garnish

Heat half the oil in a large, heavy based frying pan. Cook potatoes in batches until golden brown and tender. Drain on absorbent paper. Season.

Heat a grill pan until very hot. Add lamb. Cook for about 1 minute on each side just to sear (they will get a second cooking).

Place potatoes and lamb in a medium-sized saucepan. Add combined stock, vinegar, sugar and garlic. Bring to boil. Simmer for about 5 minutes or until lamb is cooked to your liking. Season.

Garnish lamb chops and potatoes with mint.

FERRAN ADRIA OF WORLD-RENOWNED EL BULLI HAS BEEN CALLED THE WORLD'S GREATEST CHEF. HE TAUGHT ME HOW TO MAKE THIS DISH AND IT IS AN HONOUR TO INCLUDE IT HERE. MARC SINGLA WAS THE FIRST CHEF TO CREATE THIS DISH IN FERRAN'S RESTAURANT IN BARCELONA IN 1996. IMPRESSIVE RESULTS FROM A NOT-TOO-DIFFICULT PROCESS, YOU JUST NEED THE RIGHT EQUIPMENT. GO ON HAVE A GO!

MARC SINGLA'S DECONSTRUCTED SPANISH OMELETTE

Serves: 4
Prep time: 15 minutes
Cooking time: 20 minutes

250g (8oz) diced potatoes
2 tablespoons olive oil
2 medium onions, thinly sliced
100ml (3½fl oz) double cream
3 eggs yolks
3 teaspoons hot water
salt
1 truffle, thinly sliced

Place potatoes in a saucepan of cold water. Bring to a boil. Boil until tender. Drain and reserve 100ml (3½fl oz) of the water.

Heat half the oil in a medium frying pan. Add onions. Cook, stirring occasionally, for about 15 minutes or until golden brown and caramelised. Cover to keep warm.

Meanwhile, place potatoes and reserved cooking water in a food processor. Process until smooth. Add cream and remaining oil. Process to combine. Pass mixture through a fine sieve. Place puree in a 500ml (17fl oz) siphon.

Charge siphon with gas and place in a bowl of hot water to keep warm.

Beat egg yolks and water until pale and creamy. Season with salt.

Divide onions among four martini glasses. Layer with egg yolk mixture. Carefully top with siphoned potato mixture. Garnish with truffle.

Hace mas el que
quiere que el que puede.

LAS TRES
Z.Z.Z.
PAMPLONA
España

Pietro Nocturno

EVENING SNACKS

MURCIA IS A CITY FAMOUS FOR ITS ABUNDANT LEMON TREES AND THEIR FRAGRANT FLOWERS AND FRUIT. AN INGENIOUS PEOPLE, MURCIANS LEAVE NO PART OF THE TREE UNUSED. THE JUICY FRUIT IS USED IN NEARLY EVERY DISH AND THE WOOD FUELS OUR FIRES, BUT IT IS THE DELICACY OF PAPARAJOTES THAT IS THE MOST CLEVER AND DELICIOUS USE. THE DELICATELY SCENTED LEMON TREE LEAF IS SWATHED IN A LIGHTER-THAN-AIR BATTER THEN DUSTED WITH SUGAR AND CINNAMON—A HEAVENLY EXPERIENCE. JUST REMEMBER, YOU DON'T EAT THE LEAF!

SWEET BATTERED LEMON LEAVES

Serves: 4
Prep time: 15 minutes
Cooking time: 5 minutes

250ml (8fl oz) milk
3 eggs, separated
250ml (8fl oz) water
350g (11½ oz) plain flour
finely grated rind of 1 lemon
1 teaspoon cinnamon
50g (1¾oz) icing sugar, sifted
20 lemon tree leaves
vegetable oil, for shallow
   frying
caster sugar, for dusting

Bring milk to boil. Cool for 10 minutes.

Add eggs yolks and water to milk. Whisk to combine. Stir in flour, rind, cinnamon and sugar to form a smooth batter.

Beat eggwhites in a clean grease-free bowl until firm peaks form. Fold gently into batter in two batches. Stand for 30 minutes.

Dip lemon tree leaves into batter, one at a time. Shallow fry until golden and crisp. Drain on absorbent paper. Dust with caster sugar.

Serve with custard or cream anglaise (see Basics & Sauces).

A FAVOURITE SECRET FROM ESTEEMED CHEF FERRAN ADRIA AND MY TIME AT EL BULLI—THIS IS SURE TO IMPRESS! SERVE IT IN PAPER CONES FOR A SOPHISTICATED MOVIE SNACK OR GIVE TO YOUR GUESTS WITH AN APERITIF. WHO KNEW RICE COULD BE SO COOL?

WILD RICE POPCORN

Serves: snack
Prep time:
Cooking time: 5 minutes

500ml (17fl oz) extra virgin olive oil
180g (6oz) of wild rice, preferably Canadian
pinch of sea salt flakes

Heat oil in a medium saucepan until very hot. Add a grain of rice. If it sizzles and puffs up, oil is ready.

Very carefully add rice. Cook until puffed and doubled in size. Strain into another saucepan.

Drain rice on absorbent paper. Season to taste.

The perfect ingredients
for a good chef:
respect, good attitude,
passion and happiness.

FRESH TROPICAL FRUIT ENCASED IN GOLDEN, CARAMELISED MERINGUE—IT LOOKS TRULY DECADENT BUT COULDN'T BE SIMPLER! GREAT AS A SWEET CANAPÉ OR FUN DINNER PARTY DESSERT, AND THE KIDS WILL LOVE IT. USE HALF A PINEAPPLE FOR QUIRKY PRESENTATION.

BOMBE ALASKA FRUIT SKEWERS

Serves: 4
Prep time: 15 minutes
Cooking time: 10 minutes

MERINGUE
100g (3½oz) caster sugar
125g (4oz) eggwhite
squeeze of lemon

2 bananas
1 punnet strawberries
4 figs
4 bamboo skewers

To make meringue, over a pot with water for steam whisk sugar, eggwhites and lemon in a clean, grease-free bowl until thick and glossy. Remove from heat. Stand for 5 minutes to allow mixture to set slightly.

Cut bananas into cubes, figs into quarters. Cut green tops off strawberries. Skewer fruit pieces. Dip in meringue.

Using a domestic blowtorch, caramelise meringue until golden brown and crisp.

TIPS: IF YOU DO NOT HAVE A BLOWTORCH, YOU CAN HOLD SKEWER, WITH TONGS, OVER AN OPEN GAS FLAME.

YOU CAN USE HANDHELD ELECTRIC BEATERS TO MAKE THE MERINGUE IF YOU PREFER.

I USED TO WORK WITH A WONDERFUL FRENCH PASTRY CHEF WHO HAD A PENCHANT FOR ANYTHING FLAMBÉED. AN OVER-GENEROUS HAND WITH THE SHERRY ONE AFTERNOON LED TO SOME IMPRESSIVE FLAMES AND SOME FABULOUSLY SINGED EYEBROWS AND MOUSTACHE. WE LAUGHED UNTIL OUR BELLIES ACHED—NO INJURY WAS SUSTAINED, JUST A DENT IN HIS FLAMBÉ PRIDE. EVERY TIME I COOK THIS RECIPE, I THINK OF HIM.

CHOCOLATE FONDUE WITH STRAWBERRIES FLAMBÉ

Serves: 2–4
Prep time: 5 minutes
Cooking time: 10 minutes

200g (7oz) chocolate
1 teaspoon olive oil
1 punnet strawberries
4 vanilla beans
50g (1¾oz) butter
100g (3½oz) brown sugar
splash whiskey

Stir chocolate and olive oil in a heatproof bowl over a saucepan of simmering water until smooth. Remove from heat.

Remove green tops from strawberries and, using a skewer, make a hole from one end to the other. Thread onto vanilla beans.

Stir butter and brown sugar in a small frying pan until melted and combined. Add strawberry skewers. Flambé with a splash of whiskey (watch out for those eyebrows!).

Serve skewers drizzled with chocolate.

THERE IS A MISCONCEPTION THAT SORBET IS COMPLICATED, BUT THIS LITTLE NUMBER TAKES JUST
2 MINUTES. IT WILL KEEP IN THE FREEZER FOR UP TO TWO WEEKS.

Sorbetto de Higos con Crujiente de Serrano

FIG SORBET AND CRISPY SERRANO

Serves: 4
Prep time: 10 minutes
Cooking time: 8 minutes

4 slices jamon Serrano
8 frozen figs, diced small
3 tablespoons mascarpone
cheese
2 teaspoons icing sugar, sifted
volcanic salt, to garnish

Preheat oven to 180°C (350°F). Place jamon on a baking tray. Cook for about 8 minutes or until crisp.

Place figs, mascarpone and sugar in a small food processor. Process until smooth. Put in freezer.

Spoon fig mixture into a small serving dish. Garnish with volcanic salt. Serve with jamon.

How marvelous is the feeling of melting cheese in your mouth? When Manchego cheese is still *tierno* (tender) it's almost nutty in flavour. Add some tomato marmalade to contrast the sweetness—every kid's dream. I used to eat lots of these cheese fingers as a child—my grandma used to make a lot to feed over 35 grandchildren.

MANCHEGO CHEESE STICKS WITH TOMATO JAM

Serves: 2
Prep time: 5 minutes
Cooking time: 5 minutes

150g (5oz) Manchego cheese
100g (3½oz) plain flour
4 eggs, beaten lightly
100g (3½oz) panko
oil for shallow frying
salt and pepper
tomato jam, to serve

Cut manchego cheese into fingers.

Dust cheese fingers in flour. Dip fingers in egg, then panko. Repeat twice.

Shallow fry fingers until golden. Drain on absorbent paper. Season.

Serve with tomato marmalade or tomato jam.

BASICS & SAUCES

Sardines a la Parrilla

GRILLED SARDINES

Serves: 2
Prep time: 2 minutes + 8 hours marinating
Cooking time: 6 minutes

4 large sardines (heads removed, cleaned and scaled)
4 garlic gloves, roughly crushed
1 tbsp parsley chopped
50ml (1¾fl oz) olive oil
1 lemon

Marinate sardines with garlic and parsley in the olive oil for at least 8 hours, chargrill for 3 minutes each side, season heavily.

Garnish with lemon juice and serve.

Salt and sun—that is the secret for good salazones (salted fish). A conversation method born as cheap food that ended up being a gastronomic luxury.

The Murcian coast has always been rich in three things or elements: marine salt, Mediterranean sun, both of them equals resulting in of sublime mojama. Perfect appetisers.

Mojama is tuna loin cured in the sun, no colorants or preservatives beside the healthy air that gives a unique aroma to the smooth tuna meat.

Cut into extremely thin slices and together with fried almonds. Perfect combination.

I lived in Murcia for 22 years and I don't think there was one day that I didn't eat mojama.

DRY TUNA FILLET WITH ALMONDS

Serves: 4
Prep time: 5 minutes
Cooking time: 10 minutes

100g mojama
50g almonds (Marcona if possible)
1 tablespoon olive oil
1 teaspoon salt flakes

Shave mojama onto a board as thinly as possible.

In a medium-sized cast iron pan, toast the almonds over a medium heat for about 5 minutes, stirring ocassionally. Add the oil and fry the almonds for another 5 minutes. season and serve with the mojama.

Caldo de Pollo Blanco

CHICKEN STOCK

Makes: 2.5L (8½fl oz)
Prep time: 10 minutes
Cooking time: 3 hours

1.5kg (3½lb) chicken carcases
100kg chicken wings
500g (1lb) chicken thighs
2 garlic heads, cut in half
1 small nob of ginger
20 sprigs of thyme
3 teardrops Pedro Ximenez
    sherry

Put all the chicken into a stockpot.

Add just enough water to cover the chicken.

Bring to boil very slowly, skimming as the chicken cooks.

Add garlic, ginger, thyme and sherry.

Cook gently on low heat for 3 hours.

Cool slightly and strain through a sieve.

Let the stock settle for around 1 hour then skim again and refrigerate.

Keeps for 2 days in refrigerator or 1 month in freezer.

BROWN CHICKEN STOCK

Makes: 3L (96fl oz)
Prep time: 45 minutes + 40 minutes roasting
Cooking time: 2 hours

1 chicken (2kg/4½lb)
100ml (3½fl oz) olive oil
2 garlic heads
500g (1lb) brown onions thinly
   sliced
1 bunch thyme
1 bunch sage
300g (10oz) pine mushrooms
   if available—if not use
   button mushrooms
4L (128fl oz) caldo pollo
   blanco (white chicken stock)

Roast chicken for 40 minutes on 185°C (365°F) until golden brown. Season heavily with salt and pepper.

In a stockpot, add olive oil and cook garlic, onions thyme, sage and mushrooms over a medium heat until onions are soft.

Cut chicken into four pieces.

Add cold white chicken stock. Bring to a boil, skimming to remove any fat or sediment that rises to the surface, then reduce heat and simmer for 1 hour, skimming frequently.

When cool, strain through a chinois and discard the chicken. Allow the liquid to set for 1 hour then skim thoroughly and refrigerate. It keeps for 2 days in fridge or 2 months in freezer.

It is important to add the white chicken stock cold from the fridge, The protein of the chicken will act as raft, lifting impurities to the surface. Skim impurities away to get a crystal clear stock.

VEAL STOCK

Makes: 2.5L (70fl oz)
Prep time: 20 minutes
Cooking time: 10 hours

2.5 kg (5lb) small veal necks, chopped (your butcher, will do this for you)

2.5kg (5lb) osso buco for stock (cheaper than normal osso buco)

2 pig's trotters, halved

2 onions, chunky diced

1 head of garlic

2 carrots, chunky chopped

1 small leek, roughly chopped

½ head celery, roughly chopped

10 black peppercorns

2 large oxheart tomatoes ripe

4 tablespoons extra virgin olive oil

200ml (6½fl oz) rioja

3 fresh thyme bay leaves

3 lemon tree leaves

Preheat oven to 220°C (420°F).

Divide the veal necks, osso buco and trotters equally among trays, and bake evenly to colour the meat. Check every 15 minutes to make sure that they don't burn—the stock tastes best when they are brown. Drain fat through colander.

In a large stockpot, caramelise the onions, garlic, carrots, leek, celery, peppercorns and tomatoes in extra olive virgin oil until golden brown. Deglaze with the rioja.

Add thyme bay leaves and lemon tree leaves. Add bones, osso buco and trotters on top and add water to cover.

Bring to a boil, skimming fat or sediment. Simmer very gently for 10 hours.

Leave to cool slightly and strain through a chinois.

Return stock to pot and reduce by one-third. Let it set for around 1 hour, skim through and refrigerate.

Keeps for 4 days in refrigerator, 1 month in freezer.

LOBSTER STOCK

Makes: 2.5L (70fl oz)
Prep time: 10 minutes
Cooking time: 2 hours

2 tablespoons extra virgin
  olive oil
3 lobster heads
2 bulbs of fennel, cut in
  quarters
2 heads of garlic, cut
  in halves
2 large tomatoes, cut in half
pinch fennel seeds, toasted
pinch saffron
pinch sweet paprika
white pepper
bunch basil
bunch tarragon
threads of the fennel bulbs

Preheat oven to 220°C (420°F).

Place lobster heads, fennel bulbs, garlic, tomatoes and fennel seeds on a tray and roast for around 30 minutes until fennel is very soft. Check regularly so you don't burn it.

In a stockpot, put the roasted lobster heads with the vegetables and cook for 10 minutes with the oil, saffron, paprika and white pepper. Add enough water to cover.

Bring to boil and gently simmer for 1 hour, skimming consistently throughout.

Add basil and tarragon and infuse for 30 minutes, strain through a chinois and refrigerate. Keeps well for up to 2 days in the fridge and 1 month in the freezer.

LEFT TO RIGHT: WHITE SAUCE WITH GIANT CAPERBERRIES, BLACK OLIVE VINAIGRETTE, CAVA VINAIGRETTE, PARSLEY OIL, ROMESCO MARINADE, AIOLI, LEMON VINAIGRETTE, ROASTED GARLIC, BASIL OIL.

PARSLEY OIL

Makes: 250ml (8fl oz)
Prep time: 5 minutes

2 bunches of parsley, the
leaves picked
250ml (8fl oz) olive oil
1 garlic glove

Blanch parsley leaves for 5 seconds in boiling water. Refresh in iced water.

Drain all excess water in tea towel.

Put parsley in food processor with oil and garlic or into metallic cylinder of stick blender. Process until emulsified and a bright green colour.

Strain through an oil filter without pressing, allowing the liquid to sieve naturally, otherwise the sediment will go through the oil and it won't be clear.

BASIL OIL

Makes: 250ml (8fl oz)
Prep time: 5 minutes

1 bunch of basil, leaves
  picked
250ml (8fl oz) extra virgin
  olive oil
1 garlic glove

Blanch basil leaves in boiling water for 2 seconds. Refresh in ice water.

Drain water and pat the leaves dry with paper towel.

Process leaves with olive oil and garlic. Pass through a fine sieve or chinos lined with a chux or oil filter, without pressing, allowing the liquid to seive naturally, otherwise the sediment will go through and the oil won't be clear.

SERVE THIS WHOLE AS A GARNISH. GREAT FOR SALADS OR RICE DISHES WITH TOASTED BREAD, OR MASH THEM IN THE MORTAR PESTLE TO MAKE ROASTED GARLIC PUREE.

ROAST GARLIC

Makes: 10–15 cloves
Prep time: 5 minutes
Cooking time: 40 minutes

1 head of garlic
40ml (1$\frac{1}{3}$fl oz) olive oil
5 sprigs of thyme
1 sprig of rosemary
1 sprig of sage
salt and freshly ground
    pepper

Preheat oven to 110°C (230°F).

Break garlic into gloves, leaving skins intact.

Heat cast iron pan with oil, add garlic, herbs and seasoning, toss for 1 minute. Transfer to oven and roast for 40 minutes until garlic is golden and very soft. Remove from oven, peel and serve.

AIOLI

Makes: 100g
Prep time: 15 minutes

½ garlic bulb, cloves peeled
pinch salt
1 small boiled potato, peeled
1 egg yolk
100ml (3½fl oz) extra virgin
   olive oil
salt and pepper

Using a mortar and pestle, crush garlic and salt until smooth. Add potato and combine. Add egg yolk and mix to a paste. Slowly mix in olive oil to form a smooth mayonnaise. Season.

LEMON VINAIGRETTE

Vinaigrette de Limon

Makes: 300ml (10fl oz)
Prep time: 5 minutes

100ml (3¹/₃ fl oz) freshly
   squeezed lemon juice
3 teaspoons freshly squeezed
   lime juice
pinch sugar
salt and pepper (freshly
   ground)
200ml (6½fl oz) extra virgin
   olive oil

Put all ingredients except salt and pepper in a mixing bowl and whisk until emulsified. Taste and adjust seasoning to your own preference.

TIP: RUB THE INSIDE OF THE SALAD BOWL WITH A LITTLE BIT OF FRESH GINGER BEFORE TOSSING THE SALAD AND DRESSING. IT GIVES A BEAUTIFUL TOUCH OF FRESH FLAVOUR WITHOUT BEING OVERPOWERING.

Vinaigrette de Manzanillas N'yaux

BLACK OLIVE VINAIGRETTE

Makes: 300ml (10fl oz)
Prep time: 5 minutes
Cooking time: 4 hours

100g (3½oz) manzanillas (olives)
220ml (7fl oz) extra virgin olive oil
leaves of 3 sprigs of thyme
2 garlic gloves, crushed
½ chilli de-seeded
splash red wine vinegar

Preheat oven to 40°C (104°F).

Pit olives and cook with olive oil, thyme, garlic, chilli on a oven tray to infuse at a low temperature for approximately 4 hours. Strain and set aside.

In a food processor, mix vinegar, olives and oil infuse. Season to taste.

Vinagreta de Cava

CAVA VINAIGRETTE

Makes: 750 (25fl oz)
Prep time: 5 minutes

1 teaspoon Dijon mustard
1 teaspoon sugar
1 pink shallot, diced small
250ml (8fl oz) apple cider
vinegar
250ml (8fl oz) extra virgin
olive oil
250ml (8fl oz) cava
salt and pepper

Process all ingredients except salt and pepper in food processor. Taste and adjust seasoning to taste.

SERVE THIS CREAMY SAUCE WITH PASTA OR GRILLED FISH, OR AS A DIP.

WHITE SAUCE WITH GIANT CAPER BERRIES

Serves: 2
Prep time: 5 minutes
Cooking time: 10 minutes

50g (1¾oz) butter
50g (1¾oz) plain flour
125ml (4fl oz) milk
125ml (4fl oz) vegetable stock
salt and pepper
freshly grated nutmeg,
   to taste
2 tablespoons halved caper
   berries
1–2 tablespoons double cream
juice of ½ lemon
fresh bread and crudités,
   to serve

Melt butter in a small saucepan. Add flour. Cook, stirring, until mixture thickens and bubbles. Gradually whisk in milk and stock. Cook, stirring, until sauce boils and thickens. Remove from heat.

Season with salt, pepper and a little grated nutmeg—the nutmeg will give off a beautiful aroma. Stir in caper berries and enough cream and lemon to give a loose, creamy consistency.

Serve this warm sauce as a dip with fresh bread and crudités.

This marinade will transform your humble chicken into a sizzling barbecue feast. The secret is rubbing the mixture under the skin and into all the nooks and crannies, then marinating overnight. It's also great as a sauce with grilled fish and seafood or as a sauce for pasta. The rich, red combination of peppers, chilli and nuts is so good you can even eat it as a dip with some chunks of rustic bread.

ROMESCO MARINADE

Makes enough for 1 chicken
Prep time: 5 minutes

400g (13oz) piquillo peppers
4 long, fresh red chillies
4 garlic cloves, peeled
4 oxheart or truss tomatoes
500ml (17fl oz) extra virgin
  olive oil
100ml (3½fl oz) sherry vinegar
200g (7oz) toasted flaked
  almonds
1 teaspoon spicy paprika
2 bunches sage, leaves picked

Place all ingredients in a food processor. Process until smooth.

Tip: This marinade is particularly good with chicken, but can be used with any meat, poultry, fish or vegetables.

SUGAR SYRUP

Makes: 150ml (5fl oz)
Prep time: 5 minutes
Cooking time: 5 minutes

200g (7oz) sugar
200ml (6½fl oz) water

Place sugar and water in a heavy based saucepan and heat slowly until sugar has dissolved. Bring syrup to the boil for 2 minutes.

Remove from heat and add herbs or zest if using any, and allow to infuse for 1 hour.

VANILLA CUSTARD

Makes: 1L (32fl oz)
Prep time: 10 minutes
Cooking time: 10 minutes

630ml (21fl oz) of milk
630ml (21fl oz) of cream
3 vanilla beans, split in half
250g (8oz) caster sugar
10g (1/3oz) cornflour
5 egg yolks

Bring milk, cream, caster sugar and vanilla beans to the boil.

In a large mixing bowl, mix cornflour and egg yolks together until pale.

Gradually add the milk mixture into the eggs and mix evenly.

Pour into saucepan again and cook on medium heat, stirring constantly until you have a thick custard. Remove from heat.

Cover with plastic until cooled and refrigerator until needed.

Gently reheat to use.

CRÈME ANGLAISE

Makes: 500ml (17fl oz)
Prep time: 5 minutes
Cooking time: 10–15 minutes

250ml (8fl oz) milk
250ml (8fl oz) cream
5 egg yolks
80g (2¾oz) cup sugar
zest of 1 lemon

Place cream and milk in a saucepan and bring to a boil.

Whisk egg yolks, sugar and lemon zest together lightly.

Remove milk mixture from stove and slowly whisk into egg yolk mixture.

Pour entire mixture back into saucepan, and use a wooden spoon to stir the anglaise while it heats over a gentle flame. Do not allow to boil—simmer only.

Heat until it is thick enough to coat the wooden spoon.

Remove from heat and keep stirring over a bath of iced water until anglaise is cool. If required, strain through a fine chinois.

GLOSSARY

BLACK ANCHOVIES – a small, herring-like, marine fish found in many parts of the world, but especially abundant in southern Europe. Much used pickled and in the form of a salt paste.

BOMBA RICE (CALASPARRA) – a short-grain rice grown in the Calasparra region of Spain. The rice plants grow slowly, forming a grain that is hard and super-absorbent—perfect for paella.

BOQUERONES – (white anchovies) spanish white anchovies, cured in vinegar and packed in oil.

CAVA –a type of Spanish white or pink sparkling wine. Today Cavas has become integrated with Spanish family traditions and is often consumed at baptism celebrations.

CHORIZO – a type of pork sausage, usually fermented, cured and smoked. Spanish chorizo gets its distinctive smokiness and deep red color from dried, smoked red peppers.

EDAMAME –a preparation of baby soybeans in the pod boiled in water together with condiments such as salt, and served whole.

ESCHALLOT – type of onion plant producing small clustered mild-flavored bulbs used as seasoning.

FIG VINCOTO – a sweet, velvety vinegar, with the subtle overtones of spices, grapes and prunes.

GOW-GEE – round balls of noodle dough.

JAMON IBERICO –a type of cured ham produced mostly in Spain made from at least 75 per cent black Iberian pig.

JAMON SERRANO – literally 'mountain ham', it is a type of dry-cured Spanish ham, generally served raw in thin slices.

QUESO MANCHEGO – cheese made in the La Mancha region of Spain from the milk of sheep of the Manchega breed. Manchego has a firm and compact consistency and a buttery texture.

MANZANILLA – a small, green olive, with a thin skin. It is one of Spain's finest varieties of olives and the most widespread variety in the world.

MOJAMA – filleted salt-cured tuna made using the loins of the tuna by curing them in salt for two days. Usually served in extremely thin slices with olive oil and chopped tomatoes or almonds.

MORCILLA – (blood sausage) stuffed with pig's blood, rice, onions and spices.

ÑORAS – a small, round and red pepper from Murcia in Spain, dried in the sun. It has a sweet flavour.

HEIRLOOM TOMATOES – a cultivar of tomato grown from older plant stock. The fruit retains a distinctive shape, colour and flavour.

OXHEART TOMATOES – a large, old-fashioned, very fragrant heirloom tomato . They come in many varieties, shapes and sizes.

TRUSS TOMATOES – a tomato ripened on the vine.

PANCETTA – an Italian bacon cured with salt and spices such as nutmeg, pepper and fennel, but not smoked, used to flavour sauces, pasta, etc.

PANKO – Japanese flaky breadcrumbs made from bread without crusts and used as a crunchy, crispy coating for frying food.

PINK SHALLOTS – Related to the onion, the flavour of a shallot is much milder and sweeter than an onion. Pink shallots have a pink skin, a crisp texture and a more pungent flavour.

PIQUILLO PEPPERS –a variety of chilli traditionally grown in Northern Spain. Its name is derived from the Spanish term for 'little beak'. They are roasted over embers, which gives them a distinct sweet, spicy flavour.

RIOJA – a Spanish wine named after the town of La Rioja in Spain. Rioja wines are normally a blend of grape varieties and can be either red, white or rose.

First published in Australia in 2010 by
New Holland Publishers (Australia) Pty Ltd
Sydney • Auckland • London • Cape Town

www.newhollandpublishers.com

The Chandlery Unit 114 50 Westminster Bridge Road London SE1 7QY UK
1/66 Gibbes Street Chatswood NSW 2067 Australia
Wembley Square First Floor Solan Road Gardens Cape Town 8001 South Africa
218 Lake Road Northcote Auckland New Zealand

A catalogue record of this book is available at the British Library
and the National Library of Australia.

ISBN: 9781742575438

Publisher: Diane Jardine
Publishing manager: Lliane Clarke
Designer: Emma Gough
Cover design: Lorena Susak
Production director: Olga Dementiev
Printer: Toppan Leefung Printing Limited

Photography: Karen Watson Photography
Stylist: Trish Heagerty
Recipe testing: Kellie-Marie Thomas
Props: Design Mode International, Mud Australia.
Tiles supplied by Sourceress.

Follow New Holland Publishers on
Facebook: www.facebook.com/NewHollandPublishers

UK £14.99
US $24.99